Mentorship
PRIMER

PETER LANG
New York • Washington, D.C./Baltimore • Bern
Frankfurt am Main • Berlin • Brussels • Vienna • Oxford

Carol A. Mullen

Mentorship
PRIMER

PETER LANG
New York • Washington, D.C./Baltimore • Bern
Frankfurt am Main • Berlin • Brussels • Vienna • Oxford

Library of Congress Cataloging-in-Publication Data

Mullen, Carol A.
Mentorship primer / Carol A. Mullen.
p. cm.
Includes bibliographical references and index.
1. Mentoring in education—United States. 2. Mentoring in education—
Social aspects—United States. I. Title.
LB1731.4.M84   370'.71'5—dc22   2004022832
ISBN 0-8204-7630-7

Bibliographic information published by **Die Deutsche Bibliothek**.
Die Deutsche Bibliothek lists this publication in the "Deutsche
Nationalbibliografie"; detailed bibliographic data is available
on the Internet at http://dnb.ddb.de/.

Cover design by Lisa Barfield

© 2005 Peter Lang Publishing, Inc., New York
275 Seventh Avenue, 28th Floor, New York, NY 10001
www.peterlangusa.com

All rights reserved.
Reprint or reproduction, even partially, in all forms such as microfilm,
xerography, microfiche, microcard, and offset strictly prohibited.

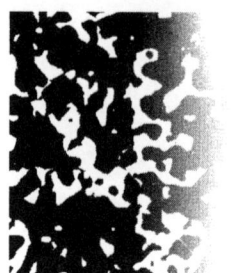

Table of Contents

1	Introduction	1
2	Foundations of Mentorship	29
3	Technical Mentoring	51
4	Alternative Mentoring	71
5	Conclusion	101
	References and Resources	111

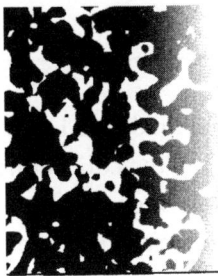

CHAPTER ONE

Introduction

Accountability expectations
professional standards for performance and conduct that are externally imposed and internally generated

Mentorship
an educational process focused on teaching and learning within dyads, groups, and cultures

Mentoring is a precious resource that has been underutilized worldwide, but as **accountability expectations** rapidly take root for many professions, the widespread importance of mentoring is indisputable. Recent developments in Westernized countries have shed light on the value and practice of **mentorship** for schools, universities, and businesses. Shifting national and global contexts have produced legislative and policy requirements for mentoring; inspired sociocultural and cross-cultural perspectives; generated programs for developmentally assisting new professionals and traditionally disenfranchised groups; and much more, which makes the *Mentorship Primer* more timely. This source should prove relevant to a range of organizations and situations across learning systems.

For decades, mentoring has been a mainstay in business, journalism, law, and medicine—fields that are clinically based—serving apprentices in their academic and career goals, and personal and social adjustment to a new environment, as well as skills development, capacity building, and professional identity (Kariuki, Franklin, & Duran, 2001). After mentoring made its way into the educational and social science domains, primarily through the field of science (Paulus & Nijstad, 2003), it increasingly aligned itself with human performance and institutional reform. Specific areas of concern include career readiness, group creativity, leadership responsibility, minority support, policy initiative, reflective practice, staff development, student learning, and teacher evaluation, to name a few. Mentoring has become a "hot" topic. Its trends within public schools and universities have guaranteed the future of mentorship as an abiding **change force** in education.

> **Change force**
> educational reform in action at all levels of an organizational culture

Despite the fact that multiple complex forms of mentoring occur inside and outside the classroom, it is generally understood as a personal or professional relationship between two people—a knowing, experienced professional and a protégé or mentee—who commit to an advisory and nonevaluative relationship that often involves a long-term goal. While the pervasive view of mentoring practice as a one-on-one relational experience represents *one* valid mode, it is overly simplified. It may also be reductive and misleading because it limits the capacity of mentoring to function at the systems level where change can occur that is not only interpersonal but also cultural and organizational.

Importantly, mentoring reaches beyond individuals to nurture the potential of groups and communities to (1) actively engage in new and exciting forms of teaching and learning integral to socialization, liberation, partnership, curriculum, and instruction (Mullen, 2005); (2) cope with the politics of education through socially conscious mentoring solutions (Smith, 2004); and (3) establish **sociocultural learning conditions** at and beyond the classroom level for shaping experience and promoting experiences that lead to growth (Dewey, 1938).

> **Sociocultural learning conditions**
> the activity-setting conducive to initiating and sustaining mentoring arrangements and

Mentoring is commonly used interchangeably with *coaching, assisting, guiding, advising, leading, teaching, learning, readiness, compensation, support,* and *socialization* (Rix & Gold, 2000). These terms inadvertently highlight only particular aspects of mentoring, placing emphasis on discrete, isolated functions, not on more comprehensive enterprise and commitment. Further, while the educational literature as a whole reflects the greater picture of mentoring, researchers—as well as leaders, policymakers, and practitioners—primarily focus on the mentoring and induction of both preservice teachers (Maynard, 2000) and inservice teachers (Portner, 1998, 2002). In addition, attention is gradually accommodating prospective and practicing administrators and their issues of adaptation and leadership (Crow & Glascock, 1995). Issues of mentoring for dissertation candidates (Piantanida & Garman, 1999) and for junior professors (Johnson-Bailey & Cervero, 2004) are two primary areas of interest in higher education.

This overall disequilibrium in the area of mentoring is reflected broadly in educational systems and more specifically in public school culture. At best, mentoring programs and relationships in schools usually connect seasoned educators and beginning teachers (Smylie, 1997) and, less frequently, principals and new teachers (McDaniel, 1999). While the preparation of student teachers, and to some extent aspiring leaders within university programs, has coverage, overlooked areas of mentoring include the cultivation of inservice teacher leaders as well as beginning and prospective administrators among current staff (Bingham, Finney, & Hood, 2000). To this list of neglected parties, we can also add the ongoing professional development and retention of practicing school leaders (Betty Coxe, Deputy Chancellor for K–12 Public Schools, June 18, 2004, "Principal Leadership Standards," Florida Association of Professors of Educational Leadership, Tampa, Florida).

The imbalance reflected in the educational literature helps to explain why mentoring continues to have an uneven focus in practice. The exclusion of a large number of professionals and students as mentoring beneficiaries in school systems has led to stagnation, attrition, and dissatisfaction for many in addition to low morale and burnout. The national shortage of inservice school practitioners is estimated to be 30–50% for teachers (Lind,

> **Comentorship**
> individuals or groups proactively engage in reciprocal teaching and learning and transform power structures to honor egalitarianism

> **Democratic decision making**
> groups representative of organizational members, including learners, participate in significant decision making through team building, goal setting, problem solving, delegating, assessing, and resolving conflict

> **Group learning**
> a formal or informal experience of mentoring wherein the team or committee acts as a mentor in helping all members develop the desired knowledge and/or skills toward a common goal or vision

> **Shared leadership**
> also shared governance and collaborative decision making, either a single leader distributes power and authority to a professional body, or a team functions more democratically, sharing leadership among a larger body that includes students of all ages

2003) and 40% for principals (Borja, 2001). However, Darling-Hammond and Sykes (2003) contend that there is no overall national shortage of qualified teachers per se but rather an insufficient number drawn to low-income school-communities serving minority students. Whether there is a widespread shortage of professional mentors or a concentrated shortage within areas of high need, the call for more adaptive, healthy, and sustaining mentoring organizations is undeniable. Democratically-oriented conditions that foster "collective authority" (Meyer, 2002, p. 37), "networks of responsibility" (Kelehear, 2003, p. 45), and "teamwork and team building" (Mullen, 2004, p. 156) can aid school leaders in this vision, and these ideas are applicable to other professional domains as well.

We will explore collaboration, **comentorship, democratic decision making, group learning**, and **shared leadership**, all of which represent nontraditional ideologies of mentoring. Contemporary best practices of mentoring include cohort learning (formal and informal), cross-cultural mentoring, inquiry/writing groups, learning communities, mentor-based programs, peer coaching and learning, professional activism, school–university partnership, staff development, and telementoring and e-mentoring. Each form contributes new stances for remedying the perceived drawbacks of traditional mentoring relationships, supporting issues of quality in learning and performance, and grappling with the complex nature of evolving human and organizational structures. We will also learn about dominant models, emergent alternatives, contextual realities, cultural constructs, diversity issues, and educational policies associated with mentoring.

A driving force behind this book is to raise awareness about how mentoring can become an even more potent force for making our educational thinking conscious and action deliberate. Also presented are various alternatives for developing or transforming mentoring relationships, programs, and cultures, which function flexibly as frameworks for and solutions to educational problems. In much the same way that school culture, while not necessarily visible to outsiders or even insiders, has been exposed as a powerful force that continually shapes the quality of our experiences (Lick, 1999b; Lind, 2003), mentoring can be construed as being always "there." This ubiquitous energy (sometimes creative, at other times destructive) that connects humans, reforms values, and affects decisions and actions—which are in part influenced by our previous schooling and life experiences—contributes to the future of our institutions, communities, and societies.

Mentoring contexts and relationships benefit from ideological guidance that underlies situations ranging from the traditional or dominant (e.g., supervision) to the contemporary or emergent (e.g., peer learning). Mentoring can also serve to facilitate desirable goals, positive change, and human possibility through such well-established ideas as lifelong learning. The concept of **lifelong mentoring** extends beyond self-actualization of individuals to embrace groups, organizations, and global systems. It views curriculum as an integral part of the developmental and life cycles of human and organizational systems (Mullen & Kealy, 1999). Conversely, mentoring that is of a strictly rhetorical nature protects the status quo—that is, the way things already are—counteracting development or change. Or, even worse, it is used as a tool for exploiting vulnerable Others via ulterior motives and concealed agendas. One cannot assume, however, that only traditional mentoring is susceptible to such negative scenarios or that alternative mentoring is somehow automatically exempt.

Mentorship is viewed herein within various educational contexts and from different ideologies. The primer frames the essential philosophical, historical, and epistemological foundations of mentoring. Anyone searching for guidance in their own professional and academic domains will benefit from reading this book, complete with glossaries, references, and resources. The theories and applications discussed accommodate K–12 public schools and universities as well as businesses and corporations. However, this text favors mentoring in education as it relates to the work of teachers and students in addition to leaders and scholars. Some of the broader sociopolitical forces that act upon schools and universities are also

> **Lifelong mentoring**
> continually seeking, finding, and reconstructing mentoring and comentoring relationships

included. The issues we will study of teacher and administrator development and preparation extend to cohort groups within undergraduate and graduate schools of education and include doctoral mentoring. The theories and practices of mentorship will be valuable for instructors and students in both college and university classrooms, as well as for leaders engaged in **restructuring efforts** within higher education and public school systems.

> **Restructuring efforts**
> educational reforms to effect systemic change in policy, leadership, collaboration, and instructional mentoring

Before continuing with the description of the foundations of mentorship and then technical as well as alternative mentoring, four core areas that provide a context relevant to these overarching themes will be briefly covered: mentoring and culture, mentoring and policy, mentoring and curriculum, and mentoring and relationship.

Mentoring and Culture

Mentoring has yet to be fully integrated within our organizational roles and lives as educators, systems thinkers, and democratic workers (Hargreaves & Fullan, 2000). It is time to develop highly supportive mentoring cultures and to transform how we teach and learn as mentors and protégés alike in our academic and professional lives. If mentorship is to achieve a higher level of potency in education and society, it will need to be developed into synergistic whole-school cultures, ideally involving everyone in student learning, reflective practice, professional development, and, importantly, shared governance and democratic decision making (Lick, 1999b; Mullen & Graves, 2000). We must realize, however, that this challenge will not be easy, as has been acknowledged time and time again for school leadership: "Of all the efforts effective principals undertake to support new teachers, building and sustaining a supportive school culture may be the most elusive" (Carver, 2003, p. 8).

A similar holistic culturing movement has been envisioned from within the higher education domain for developing professionals. This favors the creation of new undergraduate and graduate programs and curricula that integrate learning communities and other mentoring strategies. Around the country, diverse students, faculty, and practitioners are working closely together to combat isolation through collaboration, exploration, and inquiry (e.g., Horn, 2001; Mullen, 2005; Twale & Kochan, 2000) and across the boundaries of school, university, and community.

Previously labeled "compensatory support for the once-excluded," mentoring is now identified as essential to the academic and professional success of university students (Gross, 2002, p. 2; see also Nyquist & Woodford, 2000). Within the K–12 public school context, teacher induction (Portner, 2002) and, increasingly, administrator training (Malone, 2001) are considered fundamental to any mentoring environment. In higher education systems, while some doctoral students relate that their mentoring (and advising) relationship is "the single most important element in graduate education," many have appraised it as "the most disappointing relationship" (Henrich, 1991, p. 515). Nyquist and Woodford's (2000) large-scale U.S. study arrived at similar conclusions: More than 375 doctoral students reported ineffectual mentoring from their dissertation supervisors. Furthermore, an international study of 139 new graduates found that support from mentors for publishing their doctoral research was lacking (Dinham & Scott, 2001).

Without a cultural approach to mentoring that is supported colleges and departments and reinforced by leaders who are compensated for time and expertise, mentoring is left to chance (Mullen, 2005). The entire culture of doctoral education is consequently in need of serious rethinking and change: "How can we re-envision the Ph.D. to meet the needs of the society of the 21st century?" (Nyquist & Woodford, 2000, p. 2).

Rebuilding academic and workplace cultures for equity and access can enrich opportunities of inclusion, participation, and advancement for entire populations of economically and culturally disadvantaged individuals. Counted among these are students from different ethnic groups and professionals struggling to acclimate to traditionally white institutions (Banks, 2000; Kea, Penny, & Bowman, 2003); early career minority faculty, particularly African Americans identified as structurally disadvantaged and exploited within hegemonic Euro-American institutions that continue to breed mistrust (Geber, 2003; Groomes, 1999; Johnson-Bailey & Cervero, 2004); women seeking advancement within male-dominated and restrictive contexts, role modeling, and psychosocial support (Packard, Walsh, & Seidenberg, 2004; Smit, 2003); and youngsters for whom poverty, unsafe learning environments, and inadequate human and social capital (e.g., role modeling from caring mentors) are serious setbacks (Payne, 1998; Sergiovanni, 1998).

Accomplishing these cultural goals will shift mentoring from isolated pockets, and hence a limited worldview, to a systems thinking approach (Senge, 1990) that grounds the work of individuals within learning communities and cross-cultural communities (Snyder & Acker-Hocevar, 2003). Such efforts will enable leaders to articulate their vision, making onsite support for mentorship visible and viable (Carver, 2003). Importantly, transformation in school and higher education cultures will mean less emphasis on **technical mentoring** and more on **alternative mentoring** (Bona, Rinehart, & Volbrecht, 1995; Darwin, 2004; Maynard, 2000).

The cultural value of mentoring can be indirectly observed or experienced in practice. For example, one Florida school advisory board of superintendents acknowledged this essential capacity for leadership. A mentor leader was envisioned as someone who "coaches to high performance," "builds relationships purposefully and leads by example," "embraces the concept of lifelong learning" and "assesses and encourages the expertise and developmental needs of others" in creating a school community that supports school mission (Mullen, Gordon, Greenlee, & Anderson, 2002, p. 168).

The development of a systemic mentoring capacity, and other important capacities for educators and leaders, requires modeling in real-world settings. Prospective teachers and principals often identify not graduate programs but other school leaders as a critical influence in their own learning and readiness for new work (Mullen, 2004).

Technical mentoring
hierarchically transmitting authoritative knowledge within organizational and relational systems

---

Alternative mentoring
engaging in shared learning, inquiry, and power across status, racial, gender, and other differences, with a vision of empowerment and equality

Although preparation programs can "teach examples of leadership behaviors," they are less likely to communicate the "practical knowledge" that characterizes exemplary leadership (Malone, 2001, p. 1). Leaders whose capacity to improve schools has been nurtured through, for example, internships and ongoing support should be better able to develop mentoring practices that support change (Malone, 2001). Practitioners and scholars alike argue for adequate opportunities for aspiring principals through longer, more rigorous internships, mentoring and shadowing practical experiences, and instruction by model practitioners (Bloom & Krovetz, 2001; *Effective Leaders for Today's Schools*, 1999).

Examining this shared view of the problem from another angle, English (2003b) is dubious that more fieldwork practice and training will in fact resolve the theory–practice gap and argues instead for "different and better theories which predict the effects of practice" (p. 228). Solutions to systemic problems can be quickly seized upon but should be critiqued to stimulate a more thoughtful search for alternatives.

Mentoring ideologies and activities can create cultural change through democratic community building. **Social justice** and equal opportunity concerns are evident when educators envision students not as mentees to be regulated and developed for workplace stratification but as empowered, democratic citizens (Kincheloe, 2004a). Teachers and leaders who focus on issues of human capital, transcending a fixation on economic prosperity and high-stakes testing (Sergiovanni, 1998), are better positioned to avoid harming student populations, translating care into student success and retention, as well as meaningful learning experiences (Horn, 2004).

Sociopolitically driven mentoring agendas motivate educators to think and act differently and in a way that is either positive or negative. A negative scenario would involve, for example, subdued anger and resentment, a covert racist response felt within predominantly white institutions that proactively exercise affirmative action in faculty hiring and in college admissions that use racial

> **Social justice**
> the search for equity and voice in the suffering and oppression of human lives

quotas (Johnson-Bailey & Cervero, 2004). In contrast, a positive scenario would involve recruiting *and* retaining traditionally disenfranchised minority graduate students and faculty. Where the psyche of faculty and institutions is recultured to accept as well as to seek diversity, ethnic communities can be embraced. "Cross-cultural interventions" in the form of faculty preparation programs that deal with trust and power issues (Kea, et al., 2003) can make a difference, especially where attention is proactively focused on diverse mentoring relationships that include mixed-race and same-race configurations (Duff, 1999).

As another example of collective action, educators can sponsor grassroots initiatives that promote organized teacher networks and campaigns (Lieberman, Saxl, & Miles, 2000/1988). These may form in response to imposed standards (e.g., school grading and performance measures) that prove detrimental to specific schools, neighborhoods, and student groups. Finally, the issue of ranking and grading all schools using the same criteria de-emphasizes contextual realities, placing struggling schools at a greater disadvantage. Teachers from lower socioeconomic status (SES) schools, for example, complain about being penalized for high incidences of student absence that are endemic to the youngsters' lives (Mullen, 2004).

Because mentoring is not somehow magically exempt from the process of socializing or being socialized in our roles as teachers and learners, the prospect of indoctrination is a very real concern that we cannot afford to overlook. In fact, indoctrination as the "underbelly" of socialization needs to be vigilantly monitored within our places of work *and* within ourselves. From this perspective, critical pedagogy keeps attention on "the power dimension" involved in all educational processes, and it also requires that we work constantly at discerning "racism, sexism, class bias, cultural oppression, and homophobia" (Kincheloe, 2004a, p. 9). African American, Asian, Latino, Native American, and other minority students continue to be disadvantaged by assessment tools that reflect cultural bias and by schools that do not teach the "rigorous academic curriculum" that will aid in the success of minority groups (Futrell, 2003, p. 358). Such liberal education takes many forms, extending to student-centered curriculum, teacher-led action research, cross-cultural communication, critical pedagogy, grassroots activism, and legislative-and-policy participation (Caputo-Pearl, 2001; Scott & Dinham, 2002; Wood & Hicks, 2002).

Mentoring and Policy

Recent changes in American legislation and school policy have set in motion accountability requirements for mentoring throughout entire systems. Since the 1980s, policy-driven change practices have co-opted mentoring and aligned it with beginning teacher support, pay for performance, career ladder, differentiated staffing, and other compensatory programs. State directives for public school systems extend the focus for exemplary "master teachers" in successfully mentoring new inductees—they are now expected to teach low-performing students at their own schools and even to physically move, where at all feasible, to low-income schools to provide critical support (Betty Coxe, Deputy Chancellor for K–12 Public Schools, June 18, 2004). While some may believe that these intensified national standards hold promise for the retention and success of beginning teachers, and in particular the academic achievement of all students, particularly at-risk groups, many think otherwise.

Since the mid-1980s, nearly every state in the country has adopted or is studying some form of teacher leadership program or policy. Opportunities for teacher leadership materialized as career ladder and mentor teacher programs, the appointment of master and lead teachers, and policies to decentralize and engage teachers in school- and district-level decision making (Smylie, 1997). Furtwengler (1995), in comparing state policies for beginning teacher programs and others involving the improvement and compensation of school personnel (such as performance pay and career programs), found that the former had a far better survival rate. From 1984 to 1992, 18 of 34 states had mandated the statewide beginning teacher programs, proving the success of mentoring beginning teachers as a policy initiative.

Unforeseen problems for the nation's schools involving beginning teacher programs have revealed the need to develop and retain master (or mentor) teachers. In addition, the high-stakes testing culture has introduced a serious dilemma for beginning teacher programs: "The issue of formative vs. summative evaluation has not been resolved in the evaluation of experienced personnel, and it appears to be a continuing quandary for beginning teacher programs" (Furtwengler, 1995, p. 5). The new role of mentor as "summative evaluator" contradicts the nonevaluative domain of mentorship and the resulting trust and confidence. Policy analyst Furtwengler asks, what are the underlying purposes of beginning teacher programs? Are they intended as a vehicle for supporting professional development and adjustment, for instance, or as a benchmark for certification and employment decisions?

Similarly, **mandatory mentoring** is an oxymoron signaling the presence of a **hidden curriculum** where teachers are *required* to mentor and make documented gains. Performance-based expectations of mentoring could increase relational energy on the part of many veteran teachers and improve overall organizational efforts, but accountability expectations may also conflict with the democratic integrity associated with the teaching and learning enterprise. Not only policymakers but also academics have observed that "mentoring practice may fall short of its ideals" (Hargreaves & Fullan, 2000, p. 50). Workplaces often treat mentoring as an "add-on" responsibility for educators that is not conceptualized, supported, or funded as an integral part of one's workload. Exceptions include release time and stipends for school-based mentors of beginning teacher programs as with California's rigorous programs and extensive requirements.

The adaptation of mentoring as a policy mechanism is not new, but it has intensified as an accountability measure for schools over the years. New changes in law are establishing an even closer fit for schools with **systems thinking** and accountability in meeting student achieve-

---

Mandatory mentoring
compulsory requirements to commit to an educational process that is presumed voluntary

Hidden curriculum
implicit messages are communicated to students about their place in school and society, both from the formal academic content and from out-of-classroom experiences

> **Systems thinking** views organizations as a complex, "living" system with underlying structures and systems thinkers as change agents who develop "big picture" frameworks for accommodating the whole and the interrelationships among parts

ment goals. Mentoring, which has been described as an organizational capacity of leadership, is infused with leading, teaching, and supervising (Mullen, et al., 2002), and is now incorporating teacher evaluation and decision making. For example, the Carnegie Forum on Education and the Economy's (1986) *A Nation Prepared* supported the role of classroom teachers as change agents and mentors in the nationwide goals for student achievement. *A Nation at Risk* (NCEE, 1983) redirected the focus on curriculum and curriculum leadership by redefining standards of excellence for teachers and schools.

Implying a direct correlation between student test scores and the quality of teaching, measures of teacher effectiveness and high-stakes testing have since flourished. The new accountability context essentially deflates opportunities for teacher growth and meaningful learning (Waite, Boone, & McGhee, 2001). The role appears to have been rescripted for teacher mentors working in American schools. As evaluative decision makers, they are fulfilling supervisory functions of the past, in charge of bureaucratic mandates—such as standardizing the curriculum and controlling teacher behavior (Glanz, 1990)—but within high-pressure testing environments with rewards and sanctions relative to student scores, school grade, and reputation. Unfortunately, mentors and leaders generally give constant attention to improving results on standardized tests and far less attention than is needed to developing authentic assessments for student learning (Mullen, 2004; Stiggins, 2002).

More recently, Bush's *No Child Left Behind Act of 2001*, one of the most comprehensive educational acts, has brought issues of mentoring—specifically professional development and collaboration among administrators, teachers, and parents—squarely into line with standardized testing and stronger accountability. An overarching, short-term goal of the Act is to place a highly qualified teacher in every classroom throughout the nation (U.S. Department of Education, 2002). The state of Florida responded by creating the Better Educated Students and Teachers (BEST) Act, which required all school districts to implement, by the 2004–2005 school year, a salary career ladder program (Florida Department of Education, 2003). This systemic initiative spearheads differentiated staffing for supporting teacher retention and instructional mentorship, requiring that instructional mentorship be aligned with a new salary model so exemplary teachers can be recognized and retained. However, the 2004 session of the Florida Senate decided against funding this program even though statewide implementation of the BEST program is nonetheless expected by 2006 (Mullen & Slagle, 2004).

Mentoring and Curriculum

Curriculum is a Latin word meaning "race-course" or "career" (Connelly & Clandinin, 1988) that, over the decades, has accumulated numerous connotations and distinctions: a single course (syllabus); a course/program of study (a list of subjects and curricula at schools and a catalog for diploma and degree programs at higher education institutions); and, importantly, the lesson plans created by teachers and curriculum developers whose job it is to follow the school district's learning objectives, benchmarks, and program designs that respond to department of education policies and standards. *Curriculum* also includes all of the planned and unplanned experiences (or general and directed learning) of children in the classroom and extracurricular, cocurricular, and out-of-school curriculum. Less familiar or more esoteric definitions extend to the broader and deeper life experiences that schooling processes shape (Connelly & Clandinin, 1988), and, even more currently, the aesthetic (Eisner, 1996), legal (Janesick, 2003), and moral aspects of curriculum development (Pinar, Reynolds, Slattery, & Taubman, 1995/1996) that, for many writing today, cannot be separated from issues of professional accountability, specifically educational standards, high-stakes testing, and authentic assessment (Flinders & Thornton, 2004).

However, the early 20th-century imprints of Franklin Bobbitt's *The Curriculum* (1918) and Ralph Tyler's (1949) *Basic Principles of Curriculum and Instruction*, both pivotal in establishing an efficiency-based scientific understanding of and value for America's curriculum field, continue in influence. In fact, the behaviorist treatment of curriculum as a taxonomy (classification scheme), which emphasizes objectives, design, implementation, and evaluation as well as measurement, training, and testing, has been experiencing renewed support through standardized testing policies and pressures (Flinders & Thornton, Preface to the second edition, 2004; Pinar, et al., 1995/1996).

Nonetheless, Pinar (1995/1996), among others (e.g., Flinders & Thornton, Preface to the second edition, 2004), sees the scholarly curriculum field as a relatively young area of study, one that remains subject to change. In a dynamic state of development, curriculum studies have been interpreted from many perspectives, among them historical, institutional, scientific, managerial, political, racial, gender, phenomenological, postmodern, autobiographical, aesthetic, theological, and spiritual. Moreover, the null (issues not covered in the official school [or other] curriculum) and hidden (covert or ideological messages underlying the overt curriculum) curricula offer invaluable frames of reference for improving education and, as concerns our focus, developing a critical, progressive mentorship (Pinar, et al., 1995/ 1996). Both the null and covert curricula, however, actually translate into the social justice curriculum according to critical pedagogy advocates, including some mentoring researchers (Diamond & Mullen, 1999a; Kincheloe, 2004a, 2004b; Kochan & Pascarelli, 2003; Sloan & Sears, 2001).

Understanding curriculum in its various guises is relevant to the mentoring landscape of our educational institutions. We benefit from keeping in mind Schwab's (1969) classic push for understanding curriculum (development and revision) at the school and university level and the concept of the practical: "The stuff of theory is abstract or idealized representations of real things. But curriculum in action treats real things: real acts, real teachers, real children, things richer and different from their theoretical representations" (p. 35).

Here's a different scenario illustrating the practical-in-action. School principals, including those within their first

3 years on the job, have been placing a higher value than previously on instructional supervision and mentorship (Mullen, 2004). Current North American studies (e.g., McCarthy, 1999) and educational legislation (e.g., *A Nation at Risk* (National Commission on Excellence in Education [NCEE], 1983) reinforce the value of instructional supervision and leadership as a top priority in the work of schools. This focus on student learning through principal–teacher mentoring potentially signals a new teaching and learning culture. Conceivably, at a time of economic expansion and growth, the primary concern of an organization should be personnel, finding appropriately and highly qualified persons to accomplish the work of the organization. However, the value placed on instructional supervision has nonetheless been maintained in some school systems around the country as a significant priority for site-based leaders despite budgetary restrictions. However, in many school systems the emphasis given to technical mentoring over alternative mentoring seems to continue for "subordinates." For example, Oliver's (2003) 2000–2002 survey-based study of the entry-level assistant principalship in Orange County, California, confirms that while principals focus more on "leadership activities associated with instruction and programs," assistant principals are usually allocated "management oriented tasks" (p. 38).

Instructional leadership involves new administrators in such practical curricular areas as faculty hiring, classroom management, teacher–student interaction, whole-school ownership of instructional support, and standardized test interpretation. Further, instructional leaders generally model a climate of academic achievement, particularly within disadvantaged sites, in the following ways: classroom visits; curriculum assistance, one-on-one and in small groups (including feedback on lessons); technology infusion; computer-based learning in laboratories; and test and assessment training (e.g., on statewide public school tests) (McCarthy, 1999; Mullen, 2004). It is essential that both new and experienced teachers who "teach to the test" in order to avoid poor student scores are encouraged not to sacrifice their ideals in fostering a meaningful, well-rounded curriculum (Bruner & Livingston, 2002).

The relationship of mentoring to instruction, instructional supervision, and curriculum leadership can be approached from several perspectives. For example, there are mentor teachers who strictly view curriculum as that which is to be effectively implemented into classroom instruction. Their peer coaching role is conceptualized to facilitate the beginning teacher's "curriculum in use" (Posner, 1992), or hands-on application. This familiar form of mentoring engagement is often bereft of critical thinking and philosophical dialogue. In this situation, the mentor–mentee pair, while engaged in observations and discussion, would miss out on two major domains for stimulating reflection and action: situating and analyzing theoretical perspectives on the curriculum and re-examining and critiquing the curriculum.

Posner (1992) mapped out three general domains of curriculum—theory, implementation, and evaluation—for institutional uses that extend to classrooms. One can imagine mentors who perpetuate technical mentoring as implicitly viewing curriculum as a transmission process, that is, instrumentally "as a form of goal-directed behavior designed to achieve predetermined ends" (Pinar, et al., 1995/1995, p. 666). In contrast, mentors who explore alternative approaches to teaching and learning have operationalized a more multidimensional picture for integrating reflection into decision-making and growth into learning (Furlong & Maynard, 1995; Maynard, 2000).

Curriculum that is interpreted as an institutional text can be developed either within the confines of the status quo or through critical democracy. School principals, teacher mentors, and university professors who strive to democratize curriculum respect the cultural diversity of their student populations and seek to augment racial, social, and gender aspects of instruction (Mullen & Graves, 2000; Pinar, 1995/1996). As they reclaim curricular practice, educators attempt to overturn transmissive notions of curriculum and leadership development but do not stop until promising solutions are found (Sloan & Sears, 2001). These may include cultural identity pro-

> **Democratic pedagogy**
> curriculum and instructional learning for students involves teachers, leaders, parents, and other stakeholders in a community-oriented, participatory effort

> **Democratic accountability**
> view of "democracy" and "accountability" not as either/or sources of conflict but as parts of a larger whole within landscapes of change

grams and cross-cultural encounters for either students or faculty.

The pervasive "quick-fix" accountability push within the United States and other Westernized countries puts the spotlight on democratic leaders and school mentors to rise to the occasion as activists. Glickman's (1998) concept of **democratic pedagogy** envisions curriculum leaders (e.g., school administrators) as those who engage schools, teachers, and students in learning that is "participatory and community-oriented." **Democratic accountability**, another liberationist view, means that mentor leaders work to blend contradictory ideologies to enhance ownership of school renewal. They may use strategies of consensus-building and teacher and student empowerment to improve the performance of schools in ways that honor local control (Mullen & Graves, 2000).

We all live within organizational systems that reflect curriculum, both overt and covert, at the systems level. Within the school-community culture, district supervisors, school principals, lead teachers, and other leaders who have a working understanding of this concept have introduced change models that affect the whole system. In contrast, leaders whose institutions reflect entrenched curricular models from the past may need ideological renewal as well as a major restructuring effort. Notably, many scholars argue that *tracking*—the common practice of grouping students on the basis of perceived differences and "ability" levels—is a socially unjust curriculum that should be eliminated from our public schools (Howe, 1997; Kincheloe, 1999). Joe Kincheloe, Jonathan Kozol, Jeanne Oakes, and Reba Page are among those who believe that tracking separates unwanted students into vocational education. Considered a form of class-based segregation that perpetuates "resegregation" (Kincheloe, 1999), tracking is associated with anti-democratic, not social justice, values (Kincheloe, 1995).

Reminded of the lessons taught to us by Schwab's reframing of the curriculum field, social (dys)functionality has been observed as a practice within schools. As one example, Oakes, Selvin, Karoly, and Guiton's (1992) study of three comprehensive U.S. public high schools found that "race and class seem to influence vocational course participation over and above achievement" (p. 61). Teachers and counselors at these schools disclosed how vocational classes were being used as a "dumping ground" for the low achieving and the misbehaving. Curriculum leaders seem to concur that the implications of this practice for the nation's school systems are disturbing but feel yoked to the status quo and hence ill equipped to take action.

Although school reform is in its infancy, there are living examples of curriculum leaders who embody the vision of their institutions as democratic places of learning. They believe that their instructional actions are not restricted to the classroom level and mandated testing and performance issues. Mentors who look to history and have read the writings of John Dewey, for example, model the thoughtful fusion of curriculum, instruction, and mentorship to propel desirable change. Some site-based leaders have even consciously adopted Dewey's vision for restructuring their schools through the curricular integration of academic and vocational education. In response to catalytic U.S. federal initiatives, namely, the School-to-Work Opportunities Act of 1994 that funded the development of exemplary reform models (i.e., Career Academies, Learning Communities, New American High Schools, and New Millennium High Schools) across the country, numerous secondary schools have successfully incorporated this whole-school view of curriculum. For example, in 2001 the U.S. Department of Education nationally recognized the John Dewey High School of Brooklyn, New York, as a "showcase" for its development into a New American High School, complete with an innovative career academy and career institute programs (Mullen with Kohan, 2002). All such reform initiatives share in the attempt to create academically challenging, career-focused instruction for overcoming dualistic school systems. In such systems, students get labeled and sorted into work-bound and college-bound tracks—a historic reality and ongoing trend that critical scholars identify as racial segregation (Kincheloe, 1995, 1999).

However, this picture of change is complex, as the school-to-work initiative has also produced varying degrees of success. The premature closure of grant support for some of these special projects has, for example, interrupted the conversion process for low-income and rural schools. Moreover, debased models of education have also risen out of the ashes. Compromising the values of a just society are documented instances involving relinquished control by schools that has enabled corporate forces (e.g., for-profit business owners) to redirect the curriculum and subject matter content (Mullen with Kohan, 2002). Nonacademic requirements have been accommodated to such an extreme in some cases that a hidden curriculum has been erroneously justified for impoverished and "slow" students who, once tracked, are prepared for vocational slots. Authors from the United Kingdom view such dilemmas involving critical pedagogy and training pedagogy as "conundrums of our own making," and they argue for "overarching curricular frameworks" (Avis, Bathmaker, Kendal, & Parsons, 2003, p. 194). Serving as an example is the Deweyian vision of integration for mending curricular schisms.

Finally, mentor leaders who engage in the change process by working through institutional–instructional issues embedded in the curriculum should have the opportunity to formally assess any initiatives introduced top-down. Hopkins and Levin (2000) warn, however, that teachers are perceived as unable to make informed decisions for curricular reform. As Clandinin and Connelly (1992) have established through their numerous works, the question of who has the authority to enact and assess school change is at issue. Teachers have traditionally been cast as mere recipients of "codified curriculum change models." As active critical mentors or "curriculum makers," teachers transcend roles as managers of government change models, especially when backed with visionary, structural, and staff support.

Mentoring and Relationship

Different types of mentoring relationships can be fostered inside or outside of educational locales. Each type and form expresses a particular ideology, preference, and purpose. The educational literature suggests that mentorship theory and practice reflect a continuum from traditional mentoring to comentoring or collaborative mentoring to systemic or organizational mentoring. Traditional and alternative mentoring encompasses mentor–protégé relationships at the individual, group, or cultural level, and they occur consciously or unconsciously and formally or informally. Relationship mentoring can even include autonomous or "self-mentoring" where learning occurs on one's own or vicariously from seasoned professionals (Tenner, 2004; Wellington, 2001).

To expand, **formal mentorship** includes a one-on-one mentor–protégé arrangement based on assignment to the relationship (Orpen, 1997) and a cohort that has been institutionalized and is led by a qualified mentor(s) (Twale & Kochan, 2000). In contrast, **informal mentorship** is spontaneous and supported through the mentor; consequently, these relationships are not managed, structured, or officially recognized (Chao, Waltz, & Gardner, 1992). Interestingly, corporate management studies have found that informal mentoring can actually yield greater benefits for protégés than formal mentoring (e.g., Blake-Beard, 2001). Few descriptive studies of informal, as well as modified or quasi-formal, cohort mentoring in education have been published but emerging research suggests that such contexts offer particular advantages and disadvantages, not unlike formal contexts (Mullen, 2005).

Mentoring relationships vary in their structure, intent, and communication style. They can also function as technical (authoritarian) or alternative (equalitarian) models (Mullen, 2000). Although mentoring relationships are not inherently authoritarian, the distinction that is made between mentors and protégés as expert and novice, respectively, can create an unnecessary gulf, exaggerating what the former knows and what the latter does not know.

Formal mentorship
an institutionalized mentor-protégé arrangement based on assignment to the relationship through one-on-one, group, and cohort formats

Informal mentorship
a mentor-protégé arrangement that is spontaneous and self-directed, not managed, structured, or officially recognized

Such institutionalized tensions existing between mentors and mentees have unfortunately sparked opportunities for power conflict, especially where the protégé is equal in intellectual prowess or is a mature learner and seasoned professional (Diamond & Mullen, 1999b; Jipson & Paley, 2000).

The idea of a mentor as somehow separate from or above the group that follows one's charge is considered outdated (Banks, 2000). More expansive concepts of mentorship in the literature include *comentorship*, a catalyst for changing traditional practices, hierarchical systems, and homogeneous cultures (Mullen, 2000; Mullen & Lick, 1999). Specifically, comentoring or collaborative mentoring is a relational or feminist value that seeks to promote diversity by bringing women and minorities into a network or culture (Bona, et al., 1995). When practiced effectively, **collaborative mentoring** promotes critical democratic community building and enables productive synergy in such forms as cross-cultural relationships and programs (Mullen, 2000). The familiar practice of *collaborative learning* among adults (which can be distinguished from *cooperative learning*, an equivalent term relevant to primary school education) emphasizes the issue of trust on the part of college and university teachers to allow "students to govern themselves in a context of substantive engagement, conversation, and negotiation" so that they can learn to "acknowledge dissent and disagreement and cope with difference" (Bruffee, 1999, p. 89).

Guidelines developed for collaborative mentoring within the context of formal beginning-teacher mentor programs place value on dynamic, high-quality relationships. Based on comprehensive programmatic review, Head, Reiman, and Thies-Sprinthall's (1992) set of recommendations, although appearing in print over a decade ago, has enduring quality and wide applicability. Included are encouragements for mentors and mentees to pursue "continuity in the collaborative effort"; "opportunities for significant and complex new role taking"; "commit[ment] to a shared vision"; "collaboration [linked to] current research and theory"; "opportunities for analysis, reflection,

---

Collaborative mentoring
a countercultural, democratic approach to entrenched exclusivity that mobilizes social equality among individuals of various statuses and ability levels

and the sharing of ideas"; and "[inclusion of] persons with previous experience in collaboration to join the district–state–university partnership" (pp. 85–86).

Comentoring models that are operationalized in higher education demonstrate professionally equal relationships and expand upon those that are exclusive. The feeling of "ownership" by or over an individual ceases, and in its place is the vision of mentorship as a relationship between persons as different but equal. Within a dynamic, interdependent network of high performers, individuals' multiple needs—from the intellectual to the emotional—can be addressed and, to the extent possible, satisfied.

Supporting this vision of proactive and positive mentoring relationships research identifies three components of a comentoring model: "comentors are close colleagues in a mutual mentorship"; "comentors engage in dialogue"; and, "comentors form a network" (Rymer, 2002, pp. 347–348). Similar to the mentoring framework provided by Head and colleagues, these elements are relevant to any educational context.

Educational stories powerfully capture the spirit of collaboration and teamwork as **synergistic comentoring.** We can feel this synergy at work in our positive relationships, creating a mentoring bond that may have a lasting effect on one's attitude, values, and work habits. Examples are available, for example, from university faculty who share highly charged, long-term writing relationships with colleagues and students. Writing teams have reported losing sight of individual contributions and personal ownership over their own material; collaborators who begin as two selves engage in creative tension and multitracked discourse, cycling back again and again and forging a shared identity that crosses barriers in status, gender, race, and age (Diamond & Mullen, 1999b; Jipson & Paley, 2000; Johnson-Bailey & Cervero, 2004).

Issues and quality of conversation in the **mentoring dyad** are central. Although only recently studied, opportunities that such interactions create for developing professional knowledge and learning relationships have been

---

Synergistic comentoring
the effort within relationships and groups to create a total effect that is greater than the sum of any individual's separate contributions

Mentoring dyad
an educational relationship consisting of two persons, the mentor (teacher) and the mentee (student)

forthcoming from American, Australian, British, Canadian, Chinese, and other scholars. Together, these provide examples of dialogic encounters through comentoring faculty dialogue (Jipson & Paley, 2004; Diamond & Mullen, 1999b), peer coaching interaction (Tharp & Gallimore, 1995/1988), mentor–novice conversations (Furlong & Maynard, 1995; Wang, Strong, & Odell, 2004), and cross-cultural interinstitutional conversation (Mullen & Lick, 1999).

Further, synergistic comentoring relationships can enable not only personal but also social situations to change. Organizational cultures that are reworked through institutional partnerships benefit from the commitment to a shared vision. Lick (1999a) describes this process as embodying "willingness—common goals and interdependence" and "ability—empowerment and participative involvement" (p. 38). It is expected that mentor leaders will possess such relational and systems learning skills and demonstrate these to their faculties and student bodies. Marsh (2000) identifies collaboration (development of high-performing work teams and learning communities) and systems building (creation of an infrastructure that supports learning, performance, and partnership) as core skills areas. Practitioners can model or learn these skills by becoming involved in as many different forms of supportive teaming as possible, ranging from co-administrative governance councils to curriculum restructuring committees to action research partnership groups.

Finally, mentors who commit to the culture of their organization, educational policy, the curriculum, and relationships can have greater potency as professionals and change agents who inspire others.

Glossary

Accountability expectations—professional standards for performance and conduct that are externally imposed and internally generated

Alternative mentoring—engaging in shared learning, inquiry, and power across status, racial, gender, and other differences, with a vision of empowerment and equality

Change force—educational reform in action at all levels of an organizational culture

Collaborative mentoring—a countercultural, democratic approach to entrenched exclusivity that mobilizes social equality among individuals of various statuses and ability levels

Comentorship—individuals or groups proactively engage in reciprocal teaching and learning and transform power structures to honor egalitarianism

Democratic accountability—view of "democracy" and "accountability" not as either/or sources of conflict but as parts of a larger whole within landscapes of change

Democratic decision making—groups representative of organizational members, including learners, participate in significant decision making through team building, goal setting, problem solving, delegating, assessing, and resolving conflict

Democratic pedagogy—curriculum and instructional learning for students involves teachers, leaders, parents, and other stakeholders in a community-oriented, participatory effort

Formal mentorship—an institutionalized mentor–protégé arrangement based on assignment to the relationship through one-on-one, group, and cohort formats

Group learning—a formal or informal experience of mentoring wherein the team or committee acts as a mentor in helping all members develop the desired knowledge and/or skills toward a common goal or vision

Hidden curriculum—implicit messages are communicated to students about their place in school and society, both from the formal academic content and from out-of-classroom experiences

Informal mentorship—a mentor–protégé arrangement that is spontaneous and self-directed, not managed, structured, or officially recognized

Lifelong mentoring—continually seeking, finding, and reconstructing mentoring and comentoring relationships

Mandatory mentoring—compulsory requirements to commit to an educational process that is presumed voluntary

Mentoring dyad—an educational relationship consisting of two persons, the mentor (teacher) and the mentee (student)

Mentorship—an educational process focused on teaching and learning within dyads, groups, and cultures

Restructuring efforts—educational reforms to effect systemic change in policy, leadership, collaboration, and instructional mentorship

Shared leadership—also shared governance and collaborative decision making, either a single leader distributes power and authority to a professional body, or a team functions more democratically, sharing leadership among a larger body that includes students of all ages

Social justice—the search for equity and voice in the suffering and oppression of human lives

Sociocultural learning conditions—the activity-setting conducive to initiating and sustaining mentoring arrangements and cross-cultural communication

Synergistic comentoring—the effort within relationships and groups to create a total effect that is greater than the sum of any individual's separate contributions

Systems thinking—views organizations as a complex, "living" system with underlying structures and systems thinkers as change agents who develop "big picture" frameworks for accommodating the whole and the interrelationships among parts

Technical mentoring—hierarchically transmitting authoritative knowledge within organizational and relational systems

Questions for Discussion

1. *Mentoring and Culture:* What are some examples of the cultural value of mentoring in practice that you have observed or experienced?

2. *Mentoring and Policy:* Accountability and democratic issues are ripe for debate. Is the new emphasis on mentoring that policymakers have conceived for improving school performance and student learning complementary to educators' own purposes or contradictory?

3. Using the lenses of "accountability" and "democracy," interpret the underlying value structure involved in the steps taken by President George Bush to sign into law a number of grant-funded mentoring programs (totaling $450 million over 3 years). These programs share a focus on helping disadvantaged children, including those whose parents are incarcerated. (As of August 2004, the approval of the funding request by Congress and the appropriations process had not yet been decided.) Not only schools but also faith-based organizations are welcome applicants. (Mentor: National Mentoring Partnership, http://www.mentoring.org/ take_action/hot_issues/president/ index.adp, 2004.)

4. In general, why do you think people seek mentoring relationships and some even sustain them? Do you believe that this motivation to connect with talented leaders, teachers, and others is mostly driven by the sheer desire for success or does it encompass other signif-

icant needs too, such as collegiality, counseling, or parenting? Explain with reference to a mentor in your academic or professional life and the "needs structure" that you brought to the relationship.

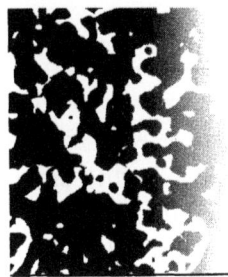

CHAPTER TWO

Foundations of Mentorship

This chapter introduces the mythological, metaphorical, historical, cultural, corporate, and philosophical influences of mentoring, all of which overlap to some degree. For example, the mythological portrait has historical, cultural, philosophical, and political overtones. In addition, this chapter examines the deep, overarching tensions of two poles, *technical mentoring* (e.g., managerial efficiency, hierarchical authority relations and structures) and *alternative mentoring* (e.g., critical democratic orientation, power-sharing professional relations and structures). While these are ideologically at odds, in real-life contexts they can either conflict with or complement one another.

The Mythological Roots of Mentoring

Many stories and even studies of mentoring allude to Homer's *The Odyssey* (translator Fitzgerald, 1998/2000), the classic Greek tale composed around 700 BC that encompasses the ancient word and image of "mentor." Odysseus, a powerful Greek from Ithaca, rises to greatness in the war against legendary Troy. Before leaving for battle, he places his young son, Telemachus, in the care of Mentor, a tutor with whom he forms a 20-year relationship. Odysseus is portrayed as sorrowful (Hamilton, 1940/1969), saddened by separation from his wife and son, worsened by not knowing their fate or they, his. In turn, Telemachus is forced to mature at an early age, both in response to the uncertainty governing his father's well-being and to Mentor's teachings.

Few may be aware, however, that Mentor is actually a woman, dressed to play the part. Athena, the Greek goddess of wisdom, disguises herself as Mentor, a respected male elder—and persuades the boy to seek news of his father. She also teaches Telemachus how to think and act for himself and assumes responsibility for nourishing all facets of his life—intellectual, spiritual, social, and professional. As a result, Telemachus develops shrewdness without sacrificing virtue, two qualities that Mentor treats as a formative part of a "higher" education (Hamilton, 1940/1969; Herman & Mandell, 2004).

Storytellers and researchers are drawn to this legend in different ways. In some cases, the tale is presented in a single sentence and tone that is politically and aesthetically flat, but writers have recently been inserting individual perspectives into the mentoring tale. In fact, the story now acts, perhaps unconsciously, as a springboard for positioning one's own personal educational platform relative to mentoring. Just as Freire (1997) encourages, readers should actively try to understand the basic concept of mythology so that they can gain insight into a writer's sensibilities and beliefs.

In one political analysis of *The Odyssey*, Herman and Mandell (2004) underscore that mentoring requires commitment to ethical agendas involving power, virtue, and circumstance. An ethical sensibility on the part of mentors is a primary concern, confirmed by a national survey of the most frequently cited personality characteristics of mentors. Doctoral graduates in clinical psychology degree programs, having viewed their long-term mentoring relationships as a good experience overall, identified positive mentor qualities as "ethical," "supportive," "intelligent," and "knowledgeable" (Clark, Harden, & Johnson, 2000).

In a more overt retelling, Packard, Walsh, and Seidenberg (2004) provide a feminist interpretation of *The Odyssey*. In their account, the mentoring experience of college females is historically linked to male-dominated relationship empire-building. They refer to how, for centuries, senior–junior business partnerships approached mentoring as a one-way, downward process in the transmission of authoritative knowledge. They argue that the import of this corporate model of mentorship into education has perpetuated significant barriers against women, partly through the limiting structure of the hierarchical dyad. Interestingly, they refer to Mentor not as a disguised female but as a male guide. Nonetheless, just as this myth relays, females have sometimes had to camouflage themselves to fit into a world not of their own making.

In yet another account, the authors confront what is considered a covert message. Diamond and Mullen (1999b) present the father not as a brave and sorrowful figure but rather a "wandering" and "erring" one. They cite that Odysseus had delegated authority to another (presumed) male (Mentor) to educate his son and protect his household. This potential ruse, as they see it, serves as a convenient arrangement for the absentee father.

Unfortunately, a stereotype has arisen from the long association of mentoring with such myths: Mentors may be unconsciously viewed as wise elders whose job it is to somehow "fix" protégés who are, by nature, innocent, incomplete (as in inexperienced and unformed) beings. Critical theorist and educational revolutionary Paulo Freire (1997) referred to this phenomenon as a "deficit lens," one that buttresses misdirected desires. He identified the dangerous process of "cloning" as one such desire, when protégés feel inclined or pressured to assimilate their teacher's values and ideas, dreams and aspirations.

Metaphorical Associations with Mentoring

Mentoring metaphors
individual and systemic images of mentors and the mentoring process endemic to education

Mentoring metaphors are an integral, living part of the collective unconscious and organizational systems. Mentors as lifelong teacher, friend, and counselor are among those living archetypes that inform our concepts and practices, in addition to our expectations, of educational relationships. Here are some similar comparisons that encompass the collective, as well as the individual psychic and physical, self.

Medical Images

As Meyer (2002) attests, "the work of mentors [centers around] veterans treating novices for some ailment" (p. 29). In fact, the medical language implicit within mentoring is so all-encompassing in educational research and daily life that mentors—not unlike medical doctors, therapists, mechanics, sorcerers, saviors, magicians, healers, and enablers—are expected to produce life-saving antidotes for human systemic problems stemming from neglect, breakdown, and decay.

The idea of *cloning* one's mentor is itself a medical image. Emulation is also a force behind the notion of being *groomed* for professional and academic success, a term so familiar many use it without thinking. Freire, however (1997), considers these propensities and desires nonsensical and believes no one can emulate another, regardless of how much effort is expended. However, role modeling itself is certainly a legitimate activity of mentoring to be encouraged.

Midwifery is another medical image that posits the mentor as "the midwife" of the protégés' intellectual, cognitive, and emotional development. The term midwife stems from the Anglo-Saxon *mid wife*, meaning "with woman." *The International Definition of a Midwife* further explains "in English midwife means someone who provides continuity of care to a woman and her baby from pregnancy through the postpartum period. In French a midwife is sage-femme; a wise woman providing this continuity of care" (Association of Midwives of Newfoundland

and Labrador, http://www.ucs.mun.ca/ ~pherbert/number1, 2004, para. 4). Herman and Mandell (2004) do not discuss the implications of women mentors as caregivers and mentees as babies; rather they see the mentor (women and men alike) as role modeling in a way that is intelligent and patient.

Metaphors We Live By, Lakoff and Johnson's (1980) classic text, invites us to think deeply about the intricate metaphoric structures of our own language systems and lives. By addressing such subtleties in the way in which we form ourselves and in turn form others, we can move beyond technical or efficiency metaphors of mentorship to reinvent how we think, act, and create.

Historical Associations of Technical Mentoring

Mentorship historically involves training youth or adults in skills-building and knowledge acquisition, both inside and outside education (Merriam, 1983). Professionals in schools, universities, businesses, hospitals, and other organizational domains enact and even model the transmission process known as **technical mentoring** or, to use Darwin's (2000) term, *functionalist mentoring*.

> **Technical mentoring**
> a needs-based, short-term solution involving the transfer of know-how to apprentices within skills-building (advising and training) contexts

Functionalism

Functionalist mentoring occurs in the contexts of instructional supervision and professional development—what might be thought of as the "parents" of mentoring, perpetuating scientific, managerial roots that thrive to this day. As leading theorists Sergiovanni and Starratt (1998) explain, the origins of supervision and its school practices emerged in America during the early 1900s from the industrially based research of Frederick Taylor. Taylor and followers held a "factory" view of teachers as workers who needed to be controlled through prescriptive managerial models. Subsequently, a human relations model of supervision infiltrated many American schools in the 1930s through the 1950s but with mixed results. The new ideals were acutely misunderstood and misused. Participatory supervision was intended to empower teachers by helping them to realize their value to the school community at large, but participatory supervision soured, turning into "permission supervision" (p. 13).

In contrast with mentoring theorists, supervision experts continue to think of mentoring as a form of collegial supervision. This difference in theoretical outlook aside, in recent years the surging interest in mentoring has created a new relationship among these practices that, ironically, links mentoring and supervision as change forces. The new era that began through ardent school reform efforts in the early 1980s has reintroduced the past in the form of neoconservative or "neoscientific management." (For an elaboration, see "Corporate Influences on Mentoring" subsection.)

Generally, technical mentoring is problematic on at least two levels, as it perpetuates (1) the use of power as a cultural socializing force that results in inequities for particular groups of people (Freire, 1997; McLaren, 1994; 2001) and (2) the algorithmic reduction of complex issues (i.e., developmental and programmatic) into "how-to" problems for which step-by-step solutions are justified (English, 2003a, 2003b; Horn, 2004). The education that occurs within this context shapes, and is shaped by, a view of leader as **technocrat,** not democrat, and of society as a **technocracy**, not a democracy.

Technocrat
technical experts and technicians who wield authority within organizational power structures

Technocracy
hierarchical forces that support mentoring as unidirectional, power based, and efficiency oriented

Technical mentoring is limited in its effectiveness because it circumvents "why" and "what if" questions, the larger societal, cultural, and political picture, and especially the regulatory dimensions of its own making. Instead, it promotes an efficiency and managerially based perspective that extends to such mentoring activities as advising, training, instructing, coaching, and leading. Largely patterned after Ralph Tyler's (1949) view of curriculum development as a reductionist formulation divorced from complex human inquiry (Pinar, Reynolds, Slattery, & Taubman, 1995/1996), technical mentorship is a firmly institutionalized paradigm in American education.

Technical mentoring practices are strongly endorsed within places of academic learning and work. They are given authority through policies that deal specifically with the perceived roles of accountability in increasing student achievement, enhancing quality teaching, and improving school performance (e.g., *No Child Left Behind Act of 2001*, U.S. Department of Education, 2002). Technical mentorship manifests itself in such forms as training perspectives applied to peer coaching (Gottesman, 2000), quality assurance systems for promoting reflection on professional practice and formal evaluation (Danielson & McGreal, 2000), sequential planning and other managerial approaches to classroom instruction (Roberts, 2001), and prescriptive models of change adapted to "organizational mentoring" (Kelehear, 2003).

Cultural Perspectives of Mentoring

Technical Mentoring as Hierarchical Authority

Feminist educators, critical pedagogues, and change theorists are among the critics who argue that traditional forms of teaching and leading encourage relationships of subordination (Kincheloe, 2004a; McLaren, 1994), thus attracting criticism and attempts at reinvention. Not only are challenging questions of relational power, social reproduction, and human suffering bypassed, but also the deeper, more sustaining educational processes that hold promise for "reculturing" (i.e., transforming) mentoring (Hargreaves & Fullan, 2000).

Technical mentoring is transmissive rather than collegial in its approach to educational relationships and work; such mentors minimize risk-taking and inquiry and maximize efficiency and productivity (Freire, 1997; Herman & Mandell, 2004). As though reflecting this posture, technical mentors may ask protégés, "What can *I* do for *you?*" (in contrast with "How can *we* learn from *each other?*"). Emphasis on the importance of "managing" formal organizational roles and "structuring" complex activity means that substantive issues and human connections are downplayed. In their place, industry is valued and modeled, reinforcing the status quo and making desirable change very difficult to undertake.

Hierarchical authority structures establish conditions for technical mentoring, encouraging noncritical reflection and feedback (Smits, 1997), as well as the mediation of autocratic or nondemocratic frames of reference. As such, inappropriate "father" and "mother" transferences and power plays, particularly exploitative ones, can compound instrumental, linear processes of learning (Diamond & Mullen, 1999b). Learning contexts that are rooted within a Eurocentric male ideology continue to confront, and even disarm, large numbers of female and minority university students and faculty (Bona, Rinehart, & Volbrecht, 1995; Johnson-Bailey & Cervero, 2004; Packard, et al., 2004). Antithetically, a smaller number of empirical studies have found that women and men fared equally well in the mentoring venture and postgraduate employment placement (e.g., Clark, et al., 2000). There are few comparative studies of white majority and ethnic minority student populations, however, due to the far heavier representation of the former in the participant groups studied.

Technical mentoring, at its most effective, is limited to the demands placed on the position, meaning that mentors only fulfill their role to the extent necessary. At its worse, technical mentoring not only reflects poor performance but also is ethically thorny for all involved. Through an analysis of the mentoring literature, Clark et al. (2000) identified several major mentoring downfalls that require vigilance in higher education and professional settings. Mentors who are ethically suspect may (1) engage in sexualized behavior toward students; (2) exercise poor boundaries in the mentoring relationship and may also be too emotionally involved, and (3) steal students' work for personal credit and self-promotion. Needless to say, the reverse scenarios also occur, with protégés as predators, plagiarists, emotional dependents, and excessively unreliable professionals. These dimensions of unethical behavior, of course, are not inclusive, and individuals and institutions must monitor such issues, as they can negatively affect entire communities of students and faculty.

It appears that if we probe dynamics of technical mentoring deeply enough, profoundly dark issues will surface. Mentoring as a moral act permeates the mentor–mentee dyadic arrangement as well as faculty–student group learning. Awareness of this reality helps with protecting against and opposing unhealthy relationship dynamics so that satisfying mentoring alternatives can be generated.

Alternative Mentoring as Critical Democracy

Alternative mentors strive to make a profound difference in the development of students, colleagues, and others, and, by doing so, actively learn from others. These individuals mentor beyond the demands of their position, seeking to enhance the development and education of protégés outside the traditional supervisory or advisory context. In fact, mentoring itself has been described in the educational literature as a separate or superordinate function because it requires an "above and beyond" effort. (Pivotal studies to this effect from the 1980s and the 1990s are briefly summarized in Clark et al., 2000.)

Similarly, alternative mentors take necessary and sometimes courageous risks. For example, they support their mentees even when facing inevitable backlash from colleagues or authority figures. The task of mentors includes confronting invisible yet influential forces within educational domains that can adversely affect protégés. In addition, such mentors are genuine as well as transparent. When appropriate, they sensitively reveal their thoughts to the mentee about his or her performance, work habits, and other relevant areas, even where this may feel uncomfortable. Such mentors also actively reach out to mentees for honest feedback as a reflective strategy for improving themselves, modeling authenticity in the relationship, and modifying the mentoring relationship itself.

Alternative mentors are not static teachers and learners. Instead, they eagerly pursue or attract creative attempts at reinvention. This effort extends to the mentor-protégé relationship itself as well as the system in which the work occurs and even the broader field of mentoring (Mullen, 2005). One example is the redesign of traditional, top-down mentoring models to better serve the contemporary needs of self-and-organizational renewal. Networks based on cooperation, collaboration, guidance, and appreciation have proliferated in education and the corporate world as a result of this vision.

Finally, alternative mentors are critical democratic leaders. Their thoughts and actions intersect with social justice concepts and sociopolitical activism. Corresponding mentoring agendas focus on transforming archaic relationship and organizational structures and on creating full equality for traditionally disenfranchised individuals and groups. Notably, racially mixed mentoring dyads and those shared by female and male faculty in higher education have had significant breakthroughs. This progress has also been reported in scholarly texts for wider circles of diverse scholar–practitioners from around the world (Christiansen & Ramadevi, 2002; Kochan & Pascarelli, 2003). Such dynamic, responsive learning organizations that connect from the inside and the outside, and beyond the local community to "neighbors" regionally, nationally, and internationally, are cutting-edge innovations.

This vision of global mentoring, however, must take into account Sergiovanni's (1998) message about local community-building. This researcher believes that each institution should endeavor to practice its own version of mentoring. Compounding this, Furman (1998) has called for studies of communities that are "in the midst of diversity," including those that have struggled with acceptance. Christiansen and Ramadevi (2002) responding to such issues, present "the local" and "the global" as ever-present tensions within communities of practice and diversity as an ongoing subject of inquiry. They make a distinction between community development at the micro level—as based on exclusive efforts within enclosed spaces—and at the macro level—when community initiatives promote inclusivity through multiple partnerships—and they encourage mentoring communities to address this paradox.

Critical democratic frameworks have inspired activism and infused the mentoring arena. In particular, critical pedagogy (Freire, 1997), feminist ethics (Bona, et al., 1995), and teacher activism (Hargreaves & Fullan, 2000) have all pushed at the edges of the status quo, together creating a more radical vision of mentorship. United conceptually as a growing democratic force, alternative or critical mentoring theorists uphold the value of humanity and the equal treatment of professionals, regardless of race, gender, age, or any other differences, and within nonpatriarchal structures and lateral relationships (e.g., Bona, et al., 1995; Clutterbuck & Ragins, 2001; Darwin, 2000; Furlong & Maynard, 1995; Hargreaves & Fullan, 2000; Johnson-Bailey & Cervero, 2004; Kochan & Pascarelli, 2003; Mullen & Lick, 1999).

Further, the creation of dynamic, reciprocal, and participatory relationships is strongly encouraged in all organizations through new grassroots innovations in learning and through more formalized systems. Some critical theorists would say that all such positive evolutions depend on the changing of **power relations**, understood here as "a panoply of operations that work to maintain the status quo and keep it running with as little friction (social conflict) as possible" (Steinberg & Kincheloe, 1997a, p. 7).

Power relations
interpersonal and structural forces that function to keep systems just as they are

Constructivist
all knowledge is actively constructed by people, products of their times and contexts who are not autonomous creators but situated knowers and constituted subjects

The alternative mentoring model is sometimes consciously political in its alignment with critical democratic thinking and perspectives. Notably, mentoring theorists from such fields as leadership, teacher education, psychology, and adult development are all countering the technocratic impetus that has rationalized high-stakes accountability and consequences for schools (Amrein & Berliner, 2002; Horn, 2004). Additionally, mentoring scholars are demonstrating a sociopolitical conscientiousness and position of advocacy relative to the learning needs of disadvantaged students and faculty groups (Grogan, 2004; Johnson-Bailey & Cervero, 2004).

Connectivity
persons linked by a common set of beliefs who conduct themselves from a premise of connection rather than separation from others

Moving closer to the center of the alternative mentoring model are social justice and its **constructivist, connectivity,** and **radical** formulations. The wheels of social justice itself, as conceptualized in the mentoring literature, embrace such agendas as antiracism, collaboration, community, dialogue, empowerment, subjectivity, and transformation. Contexts of study encompass, among others, the educational world (Bona, et al., 1995), the corporate world

Radical
extreme conservative or liberal change catalyst seeking to make major reforms in society, politics, or institutions

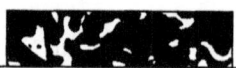

(Darwin, 2000), and the medical world (Smith, McAllister, & Crawford, 2001). Importantly, the critical democratic framework of mentoring is counterbalanced by proliferating examples of diversity and experiments in learning (see chapter 4).

Within the alternative mentoring model, radical critiques are starting to flourish, and different points of view can now be heard. For example, Freire's (1997) belief, which many critical mentors share (e.g., Darwin, 2000; Herman & Mandell, 2004) is that "a critical understanding of one's role in the world" raises ethical questions that must be addressed (p. 314). With the "nationalization" of performance-based standards for university preparation, though, teacher education and educational administration programs reify technical and procedural knowledge (English, 2003a, 2003b) at the expense of a study of **ethics**. Some critics believe that we can only hope to turn around this prevalent worldview by demanding that personal subjectivity, critical theory, and social justice come to the fore as the new curriculum in our schools, universities, and businesses. Such projects are politically radical, Freire warns, and hence threatening to the status quo, defined ideologically as the new pragmatics of "neoliberalism" (p. 314).

Another social justice issue involves the extent to which white males should be mentoring nonwhite women. Some feminists posit that this widespread type of relational mentoring should remain open to white males and that teachers should be paired with learners of both genders and all races. In fact, Dreher and Chargois' (e.g., 1998) studies of historically black universities have found that women and minorities paired with white male academic mentors can benefit from having access to the covert, long-established power structures that enable success and include compensation advantages (e.g., employment, information access, professional networking, salary, and visibility). These researchers infer that "cross-race developmental relationships" (p. 402) should therefore be extended beyond academic institutions to workplaces. Within this worldview, the controversial form of senior

---

Ethics
questions of concern to all human beings in the conduct of daily life

white manager–minority newcomer relationship is endorsed. Because institutions still struggle to sponsor equitable systems of socialization and learning for women and minorities, it is therefore believed that any insider access to the power grid can prove somewhat advantageous for the mentee.

However, some radical feminist critics provide a contradictory viewpoint. They counter that constrictive access for disenfranchised individuals and groups within organizational cultures is the more pressing issue, not whether white males should mentor them. Darwin's (2000) concept of the "cycle of power" is a case in point. She claims that cultural socializing forces operate within the workforce wherein power is recycled between male mentors and protégés as part of a closed-life system. In this worldview, career advancement and professional identity development are protected investments, and many qualified women and minorities continue to be denied key executive roles and decision making. Duff's (1999) close alliance with corporate America paints a more hopeful picture of a world that is changing for the better, with positions of privilege and power afforded to women of many different races. Woman-to-woman mentoring embraces entry-level and executive business positions as well as age- and race-based agendas, both inside and outside corporate boundaries.

Corporate Influences on Mentoring

Through Educators' Eyes

In Westernized countries, the educational system is a place where conservative and corporate forces coalesce to produce managerial systems of accountability. These, in turn, significantly mold supervisory (and hence mentoring) practices (Scott & Dinham, 2002). Critical thinkers believe that technical standards in education debase human passion and learning. By reifying objectivity and knowledge over subjectivity and intuition, logical–scientific thinking is thought to dominate school culture and teacher morale. As Kincheloe (2004a) argues, even where individuals exhibit "agency" as independent thinkers, tradition and its constant reinvention make certain practices seem natural and inevitable.

Educational critics believe that the ardent school reforms of the past 25 years have fundamentally changed American schools into neoconservative think-tanks overly concerned with scientific approaches to teaching and learning. According to Sergiovanni and Starratt (1998), the traditional managerial interest in "control, accountability, and efficiency" has resurrected a far more impersonal approach. Now, national- and state-level efforts to control teachers involve "standardized criterion-referenced testing" and "mak[ing] public the scores by class and school" (p. 14). Sergiovanni and Starratt indicate that such changes drastically affect school climate, which extends to mentorship: "In neoscientific management impersonal, technical, and rational control mechanisms substitute for face-to-face close supervision" (p. 14).

One implication of mentorship is that it should be redirected to focus on school ownership and specifically on practitioners' collaborative learning and decision making. Imagine the challenges involved in curriculum ownership for school leaders and teachers for whom authenticity is at odds with standardization and commercialization. Teachers, in particular, acknowledge that "the longest distance in the world is between an official state curriculum policy paper and what goes on in a child's mind" (Schrag, 1998, p. 73).

Many critics in mentoring, leadership, and other educational fields also believe that this heavy reliance on externally imposed authority overshadows the integrity of teachers' work. The human dimensions of supervision, such as teacher morale, job satisfaction, and reward structures, consequently suffer. Evaluation methods endorsed through high-stakes testing policies overly rely on "so-called objective data collection" for assessing predetermined, not emergent, task behaviors. This has the unfortunate effect of forcing practitioners into the practice of simplifying and even distorting complex patterns of curriculum development and classroom interaction in order to conform to normative expectations (Pinar, et al., 1995/1996, p. 728). Because of such trends, state-mandated forms of educational supervision have been characterized as "primitive scientism" (Pinar, et al., p. 728) or behaviorism "revamped." It is within this climate that mentoring models and processes are being aggressively streamlined, if not repackaged, for alignment with accountability goals that include quality teaching, assessment, and credentialing (Portner, 2001).

Just as "America's corporate producers of kinderculture are the most influential pedagogues and policymakers" (Steinberg & Kincheloe, 1997b, p. 10), the same can be said of the high-stakes testing and accreditation cultures. Governmental regulations over education have been more and more influenced by highly intricate acts of corporate control. Commercialization of the curriculum is a significant force driving the process of evaluation for school performance that, in turn, presides over mentoring models and programs. This chain reaction has reintroduced, and with vigor, technical–rational administrative approaches to learning, mentoring, and evaluating. These externally imposed methods standardize not only student learning through testing policies but also teacher performance through accountability to their students' test scores.

The scope of mentoring between teachers and students and especially among teachers themselves and in relation to such stakeholder groups as parents is also altered in the case of schoolwide improvement efforts. For example, teachers who undertake school planning for the purposes of accreditation are provided very limited roles of partnership within a transmissive reform culture that privileges standardized measures and permits corporate control over curricular and mentoring processes. National policy mandates prohibit school teams from creating their own guidelines for addressing systemic change and even from developing their own study instruments and from tallying the results. Pre-set standards, compounded by for-profit instruments, external evaluators, and other variables, typify parameters that school teams must contend with (and may find useful) as they endeavor to transform accreditation processes into purposeful self-studies (Mullen, with Stover & Corley, 2001). Such top-down, outside-in forces emanate not only from multinational for-profit corporations but also extend to such nonprofit organizations as the National Study of School Evaluation (NSSE) and the Southern Association of Colleges and Schools (SACS).

It must be remembered that schools and corporations are fundamentally different for many reasons. For one thing, markets value efficiency and self-interest, in contrast with democracies that value complexity and the collective (Sergiovanni & Starratt, 1998). Yet, market forces have been endorsed at the highest levels of government through policymaking initiatives to recreate schools as competitive markets. Just as sports have been thoroughly commercialized over time, so too are schools being subjected to this process and with mounting zeal. Schools have been forced to function more as organizations or extended markets rather than as educational communities where practices of democratic learning happen (Sergiovanni, 1998). When such communities do exist, the spotlight on genuine teacher development, collaborative mentorship, and student learning can fade unless these can be shown to have relevance for raising student test scores and enhancing school image (DuFour & Eaker [1998] noncritically make these points).

Corporate control, then, affects the school ownership process and encourages profiteering from school improvement associations and politically affiliated companies that have created lucrative markets around statewide tests. Such breaches in ethics have essentially merged pedagogy with the forces of capitalism, a pattern observed by McLaren (1999): "It is impossible to examine educational reform in the United States without taking into account the continuing forces of globalization and the progressive diversion of capital into . . . financial . . . channels—what some have called 'fat cat capitalism'" (p. 277).

Critical theorists provide additional evidence along these lines. Notably, most of the thousands of interest organizations active in Washington, D.C., are corporate sponsored, enjoying a monopoly on shaping congressional and public opinion in support of business agendas (Steinberg & Kincheloe, 1997a, 1997b). Policymakers attach the promise of merit for schools that produce high scores and sanctions for those that do not. Scott and Dinham (2002) write that "carrots" and "sticks"—rewards and punishments—are widely used at all levels of the educational system in Australia, the United Kingdom, the United States, and elsewhere, placing responsibility for quality and educational improvement squarely on the shoulders of our schools.

Mentoring summons notions of civic virtue and goodness in people's minds and so it has proven useful as a political tool. Rhetorically exploited, mentoring concepts (e.g., "instructional mentorship," "mentor teacher," "mentoring for success") have been coopted and aligned with the goals of accountability. As one effect, legislative policymaking has ironically resurrected technical forms of mentoring in a contemporary guise. Further, the recent cultural practice of sorting classroom teachers into categories of quality that draw upon, as one marker of achievement, mentoring expertise and experience (Mullen & Slagle, 2004) is compounded by the fact that not all school leaders may endorse such approaches to characterizing teacher effectiveness. Site-based and district-level practitioners, however, are rarely represented as legislative liaisons at the policymaking table (Mullen, 2002).

From a less skeptical perspective, such legislative trends might seem progressive, signaling an overdue honoring of the instructional mentorship of teachers by the American government. Many are hopeful that national and state initiatives will "engineer" a new movement that both respects and rewards school practitioners who, by committing to collegial mentoring responsibilities, assume a more formally recognized leadership status (Mullen, 2004). Similarly, optimists believe that as work arrangements change through educational and corporate restructuring and domestic and international expansion, mentoring practices will be forced to become more diverse (Eby, 1997).

Through Corporate Representatives' Eyes

The mentoring school portrait provided herein is obviously biased in some ways. Accordingly, influential voices of dissent can be constructed from four governmental and corporate domains: educational policymakers; corporate executives and researchers; authors of self-improvement studies and guides; and educators who partner with corporations and businesses. This book offers various perspectives on educational policymaking at the federal, state, and local levels (see, e.g., chapter 1) and on educational partnerships with businesses that include academic–vocational programs (see chapter 3). In this subsection, then, we will turn our attention to the other two dissidents—corporate executives and researchers as well as self-improvement authors.

Corporate executives and researchers. As a spokesperson of the corporate culture, Duff (1999) gives numerous inspiring examples of how woman-to-woman mentoring has produced various types of robust groups across the United States. Among the corporations that she has personally investigated is New York-based Kodak Company, which sponsors diversity among its employees. Kodak's mentoring networks include the Veterans Network of Kodak Employees, Native American Council, and African-American Network, Hispanic Organization for Leadership in America, and Lamba (for gay employees) (see Kodak Company, Community Affairs, http://www.kodak.com/US/en/corp/community.shtml, 2004). The Women's Forum of Kodak Employees is noteworthy because it focuses on "project management and other leadership responsibilities that give [members] experience and visibility" (Duff, p. 141).

Kathy Kram (1985/1988), professor at the Boston University School of Management, is a pioneer researcher of work-based mentoring relationships in organizations. Her research laid the foundation for the mentoring field with the theory that two major functions define healthy developmental relationships: psychosocial (already described) and career. Kram's research expands upon Daniel Levinson's (1979) classic 10-year study of human development and the life cycle that combined a career and training perspective with blended concepts from psychology and the social sciences.

Levinson's work is limited to four case studies of males, together construed as representing life's phases from early adulthood to transitional early life to mid-life. However, Levinson appreciates that mentoring is multifaceted, and so his work supports a view of both male and female mentors as teachers, sponsors, developers (of skills and intellect), and guides. Interestingly, the current emphasis in schools on quality teaching and recertification, as well as peer coaching, may have been in part influenced by this collaborative work, which gives overdue attention to the professional development cycle of seasoned professionals.

Self-improvement authors. Mentoring from a self-improvement perspective has been extremely popular with readers for decades. Produced for mass consumption, *self-help texts* target topics of great public appeal and are marketed as step-by-step programs for more complete living. Blockbuster sellers feature Carnegie's (1936/1998) *How to Win Friends & Influence People* and Covey's (1989) *The Seven Habits of Highly Effective People*. Such mentoring classics have helped launch multimillion "big-business" corporations that provide leadership seminars and other services to a variety of organizations, including schools (e.g., Dale Carnegie, http://www.dalecarnegietraining.com, 2004). These texts also combine, with relative ease, the paradigms of marriage, war, victory, religion, competition, and success, and address strategies for increasing personal and professional power with personal "growth." They target an endless litany of human frailties, among them low self-esteem, ineffectual public speaking, poor communication, and nonsystematic management.

Contributing from an empirical viewpoint, business researchers, many of whom are university faculty (and also workplace consultants), bring awareness to how mentoring can assist newcomers in adjusting to their workplace and, along with other employees, in improving the quality of their performance (Allen & Finkelstein, 2003). Studies of businesses and corporations include traditionally disenfranchised groups (e.g., women, minorities, persons with disabilities, second language learners) in these areas of transition, assistance, and performance (Duff, 1999). Many researchers believe that the success of women and ethnic minority groups within workplace cultures depends on the viability of mentoring through structured relationships that include "well-established career development systems" as well as psychosocial forms of support (Dreher & Chargois, 1998, p. 414).

Concluding on a Philosophical Note

Philosophically, mentorship fits into many different frameworks. As demonstrated in this book, it is steeped in paradigms of systems thinking, scientific and corporate management, and teacher (and employee) effectiveness as well as cross-cultural mentoring and other forms of democratic renewal.

As innovative ideas and practices of enriched and liberated (alternative) learning expand in our learning environments (see chapter 4), mentorship is outgrowing its associations with deficiency. But let us remember that antiquated notions of mentoring also live on. Notably, the subconscious view of mentors as the "be-all" and "fix-all" permeates educational cultures. Technical mentors, when fully engaged, function as top-down guides in the role as expert and teacher (not colearner) who manages the learning tasks (not journey) of others presumed barely capable. In turn, mentees must hold up their own end of the "bargain" as codependents and diplomatic receivers of facts and knowledge—commonly referred to as a "banking" metaphor (Freire, 1997).

In contrast, alternative mentors engage in and model lifelong learning and interdependence and encourage independent thought; they also relinquish control but not responsibility. Accordingly, such guides suspend their egos and support the concept of a group acting as a mentor in a way that no "expert" probably can. Recorded cases in business and education alike verify that this reciprocal process of group learning is more effective than mentor–mentee pairs. However, dyads continue to have an essential and inevitable function in many contexts, such as entry-level career induction and doctoral supervision, and they can also work as a synergistic complement to group mentoring (Duff, 1999; McIntyre, 1997; Mullen, 2005).

As chapter 3 will illustrate, technical mentoring has been built into the very infrastructure of our institutions and work. Disruptive incongruities in our worlds help explain why alternative mentoring practices have appeared, at times, to be the "flip side" of the technical mentoring coin. The overarching "paradigms" of technical and alternative mentoring view the purposes of education differently, which affects how programs, relationships, and systems will be envisioned, developed, and organized. Tensions between alternative mentoring and technical mentoring, however, remain underexplored, a gap that this book seeks to fill.

Glossary

Connectivity—persons linked by a common set of beliefs who conduct themselves from a premise of connection rather than separation from others

Constructivist—all knowledge is actively constructed by people, products of their times and contexts who are not autonomous creators but situated knowers and constituted subjects

Ethics—questions of concern to all human beings in the conduct of daily life that some theorists separate from larger moral issues

Mentoring metaphors—individual and systemic images of mentors and the mentoring process endemic to education

Power relations—interpersonal and structural forces that function to keep systems just as they are

Radical—extreme conservative or liberal change catalyst seeking to make major reforms in society, politics, or institutions

Technical mentoring—a needs-based, short-term solution involving the transfer of know-how to apprentices within skills-building (advising and training) contexts

Technocracy—hierarchical forces that support mentoring as unidirectional, power based, and efficiency oriented

Technocrat—technical experts and technicians who wield authority within organizational power structures

Questions for Discussion

1. Images of "rising" (e.g., "high stakes venture" and "falling/fallout") are used throughout this chapter. Identify where in the writing each of these images occurs and how each is used, and then speculate on the messages communicated about mentorship.
2. List all of the mentoring metaphors you can find in this chapter, and then generate a few of your own related to teaching or learning. Ask yourself which of your examples are "technical" and which are "alternative" ideas of mentoring. Did you find it possible to make this distinction in each instance? Why or why not?
3. Write a list of some of the concrete ways new mentors (e.g., preservice teachers, inservice teachers, and school leaders, in addition to teacher and leader faculty) as well as entire school communities or university programs, can become "mentorship literate." Create a context for this exercise that targets a group and setting of your choice.
4. Identify a high-stakes test or accreditation report in your locality and trace its sponsorship and development through the echelons of government, the corporate world, and professional associations. After tracing the chain of influences (use a network or "tree" diagram), share your findings with someone else. You can also use this activity (or any other in this book) as a means for teaching others.

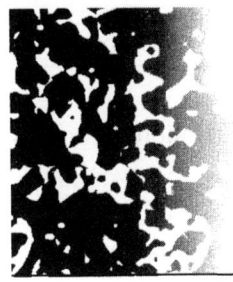

CHAPTER THREE

Technical Mentoring

While some consider technical mentoring to be an up-to-date way of socializing professionals, others would strongly disagree. For traditionalists, this approach to mentoring is viable and it is to be used in teaching, advising, and training contexts. However, many educators, including critical mentor theorists, would judge this method as traditional or passé and, depending on the situation, even politically unsound or morally dubious.

As chapter 1 describes, because advising and training represent only two aspects of the complex art of mentoring, they do not equate with mentorship. Also, student advising and training are not somehow magically exempt from the transmission of power and authority. When advising and mentoring, as well as training and mentoring, are treated as one and the same, dynamic transformative structures and processes of mentorship—such as collaborative mentoring and the learning community—struggle for visibility and impact or get overlooked altogether. As addressed in chapter 4, the rebalancing of power is seen in the field of mentoring when traditional relational practices are confronted *and* changed.

Before continuing, it is important to clarify that *technical mentoring* is an umbrella term expressed in many different ways. The concept is also reflected within socialization processes and embedded within value structures. Examples that incorporate education and other professional domains include scientific management, professional management, managerial coordination, and "managementspeak" (English, 2003a), as well as "technical standards systems," "traditional hierarchical structure" (Horn, 2004), "instrumental practice" and "technical rationality" (Schön, 1987), in addition to technical efficiency, bureaucratic leadership, managerial competency, skills-based learning, basic know-how, career counseling, vocational curriculum, and even **positivism**.

Positivism
scientific linear models that promote technical approaches to mentoring and standards and that discourage importance of context and transformation; perpetuates the belief that human destiny is inevitable

Contextualizing Technical Mentoring

While limited in scope and ideologically troublesome, many would counter that technical mentoring is helpful and necessary in a variety of settings for the support it can lend to novice professionals. Context and relationships greatly impact how individuals experience any particular form of mentoring. One should not presume, then, that technical mentoring has absolutely no educational value for those involved or that it cannot function synergistically with alternative forms. On the other hand, many ideologues would assert that the power and authority, as well as the efficiency and competitive values implicit in technical mentoring undermine the human and social values integral to alternative mentoring and so should not be tolerated.

There are many examples of the blending of the two ideologies in the literature and in practice. For example, while the peer coaching model that Gottesman (2000) describes reifies training rituals for staff development, teachers are encouraged to create their own meaning as cofacilitators. By doing so, they can take the journey of turning their schools into productive learning places. The procedural steps and checklists this former school principal outlines—such as the three phases of peer coaching, which are peer watching, peer feedback, and peer review—have a larger purpose. These motivate adults of equal status and of entry status to commit to growth-related opportunities.

Volumes such as Zachary's (2000) mentor guide theorize that such coaching mechanisms can actually be congruent not only with learning partnerships but also with a **learner-centered mentoring paradigm.** This model can originate in technical mentoring and it can potentially overcome a **mentor-driven paradigm.** Such popular guidebooks for the field attach great value to skills-based mentoring and relationships steeped in positional power. To the extent that countercultural modes of mentoring are recognized, these two "paradigms" appear to coexist and do so without conceptual tension. However, it is important to note that the claims in such manuals are usually based only on anecdotal evidence, typically in the school-based roles of teacher and leader. Empirical research and radical thinking are not hallmarks, then, of mentoring manuals.

Danielson and McGreal's (2000) text on teacher evaluation acknowledges, in keeping with some of the mentoring literature, that mentors can function more formally as guides who may be assigned to a relationship; alternatively, in the role of peer coaches they act as nonjudgmental, collegial support systems. Both types of "mentors" promote professional inquiry through, for example, self-reflection and experimentation. They use such methods as observation and feedback to assist beginning as well as experienced teachers in situations that include retooling for new subjects and grade levels.

Mentor teachers are *not* supervisors or formal evaluators, yet their feedback can and often does have an evaluative dimension. Increasingly they have been utilized in several evaluative capacities, not only in helping teachers prepare for formative assessments at their schools and for national-level teaching boards but also, in some instances, actually assisting principals in assessing the promotion and continuing employment of teachers (Danielson &

Learner-centered mentoring paradigm
a worldview of mentor-mentee relationships grounded in shared discovery and learning, with mentors cast as facilitators or partners

Mentor-driven paradigm
a traditional standard for authoritarian relationships that assume a one-way knowledge conduit and the mentee's passivity, obedience, and mastery of learning

McGreal, 2000). North Carolina continues to struggle with problems similar to those of other states that integrate requirements in their mentoring programs. For example, the state has long required its mentoring programs to use the North Carolina Teacher Performance Appraisal Instrument (TCPAI), an instrument for assessing student teacher competencies. As reported, "such a role often brings mentors dangerously close to compromising their assistance role and the safety required for risk taking, candid and open discussion of problems, and learning." It is recognized that "This is especially a potential problem in North Carolina as the evaluations are used to determine future employment and eligibility for state teacher certification" (The Story of State-Mandated Mentoring in North Carolina, www.teachermentors.com, 2004).

Mentorship and supervision are subtly intertwined in such real-life scenarios, even though they have distinct purposes and serve different functions within educational systems. Mentoring school consultant Hal Portner (2001) states that the trend in this direction can be largely attributed to the impact "powerful national education organizations" (p. 96) have had on school districts, citing the rapid implementation of Peer Assistance and Review (PAR) programs throughout the nation's schools. PAR programs align supervision and evaluation with mentoring, as encouraged by the 1998 AFT/NEA [American Federation of Teachers/National Education Association] influential handbook, *Peer Assistance and Peer Review*. A remedy is to consider the preliminary success of Connecticut's separation of the mentor's role in its PAR programs from that of formal evaluators; the designated mentors help mentees prepare for review but are not involved in the evaluation process beyond this.

The evaluative function of mentoring also extends to classroom learning. It permeates teacher–student relationships and is, in fact, strongly encouraged as a tool for promoting open dialogue about goal-setting and assessment methods (Herman & Mandell, 2004). Further, in higher education, teaching faculty and thesis chairs, in their roles as either informal or formal mentors, collectively use a range of assessments not only for assigning course grades but also for judging the merits of a student's inquiry and progress. Such situations hint at the blurred realities for mentorship. Its learning and assessment dimensions are a part of our everyday worlds, yet the intensification of standards for improvement and evaluation has amplified the evaluative aspects of mentoring. This academic change reflects a significant legal reform. The **No Child Left Behind Act of 2001** (U.S. Department of Education, 2002) has legislated accountability for student achievement, school outcomes, and professional development for all public schools in America, which has serious implications for the mentorship (preparation and assessment) of K–12 teachers and leaders.

> **No Child Left Behind Act of 2001**
> one of the most comprehensive acts pertaining to education, this federal law (signed by President George Bush in 2002) underscored four principles and goals: stronger accountability from schools for results, greater freedom for states and communities, support for research-based educational methods, and more schooling choices for parents

Traditional and contemporary paradigms that describe the world of mentoring with reference to different value structures are not always separated in practice. An example of this phenomenon can be seen in Blasé and Blasé's (2000) study of the practices of principals. Exploring how school leaders promote teaching and learning, they found that various strategies are used for impacting teacher practice, such as providing feedback in problem-solving settings, demonstrating teaching techniques, using inquiry, soliciting advice, and giving specific praise. Here, the researchers have, perhaps unknowingly, blended different ideological perspectives: Technical mentoring (i.e., demonstrating teaching techniques) appears to live comfortably alongside alternative mentoring (i.e., using inquiry and soliciting advice). For some, this blending of paradigms is "natural," whereas for others it may signal an underdeveloped critical capacity or a missed opportunity for reflection on one's own ideological orientations.

Other writings also exhibit this "unapologetic" free-flow between the contradictory ideologies of technical mentoring and alternative pedagogy. This insight into the synthesizing of paradigms is seen in texts published by scholarly presses. Take, for example, Paulus and Nijstad's (2003) edited volume, which discusses how domain knowledge (e.g., background knowledge) and creative skills (e.g., risk-taking) can be taught and, moreover, used to support group creativity. This perspective, a combination of social psychology and industrial administration, aligns a technical–rational training approach to mentoring with workgroup innovations. Scholarly texts, then, not only guidebooks, present perspectives on training that are uncritically (or naturally) intermixed with those of social transformation.

Moreover, scholars, practitioners, policymakers, and consultants merge with apparent ease the language of management (e.g., "monitoring quality," "managing conflict," "accountability safeguards") with that of empowerment (e.g., "learning environments," "relationship sensitivity," "cross-cultural mentoring"). It may be, then, that the deep semantic structure of technical language is infused into mentorship theory and practice, including its alternative languages and forms. Within educational contexts, it seems that regardless of the new possibilities for growth and change that become introduced to professional groups both indigenously and exogenously, technical mentoring scaffolds (processes and systems) have magnetic appeal.

We know, for instance, that new teachers and leaders eagerly seek promising models for improving the quality and effect of their performance, or, where overwhelmed, shortcuts to help ensure survival. Overall, these can take the form of an instrument (e.g., testing guide), a person (e.g., peer coach), a document (e.g., how-to guide), or even a process (e.g., formal support system) or program (e.g., peer coaching). Practical guidebooks for principals encourage attention to be paid to improving school culture and to offering professional assistance. The administrative managerial focus is on action for entire schools through, for example, parent communications and differentiated faculty loads as well as for classrooms, as in instructional supervision (classroom observation and documentation) and student discipline (Roberts, 2001; Schumaker & Sommers, 2001; Zachary, 2000). Such technical–rational portrayals tame or supplant, depending on one's perspective, the complexities of educational mentoring environments.

Connections to Higher Education Reform

Trends in technical mentoring also impact higher education. A growing need exists in teacher education and educational leadership programs at the undergraduate and master's level to, for instance, become standardized and aligned with the professional expectations of the field. Even doctoral education, especially within applied-knowledge disciplines involving the preparation of teachers and leaders, has been identified as a domain that must "modernize" by accommodating the current needs of the profession (Nyquist & Woodford, 2000). For decades, educational leadership programs have been seriously criticized for failing to teach concepts to new generations of aspiring administrators that are useful for "solving real problems in the field" (Murphy & Forsyth, 1999, p. 15). Lortie (1998) attests that conceptual skills—such as collecting and interpreting school data, reporting results to stakeholders, and making informed decisions based on findings—are nonnegotiable to the work of mentor leaders and therefore must be taught in educational administration programs.

Not everyone agrees that the workforce preparation of education students in undergraduate and graduate programs is the best direction in which to take these applied disciplines. Many states have adopted the Interstate School Leaders Licensure Consortium (ISLLC) and National Council of Accreditation for Teacher Education/Educational Leadership Constituent Council (NCATE/ELCC) standards for reforming and hence standardizing educational leadership preparation. An objective of the NCATE/ELCC standards committee has been to align university programs with the expectations of stakeholder groups, primarily school districts, in order to produce workforce-ready leaders. Critics, notably Fenwick English (2003a), scrutinize these nationwide adoptions by states and schools of education as "cookie-cutter" solutions to individualism (as reflected in university programs) and complexity (as reflected in issues of preparation).

Many in the academic ranks have argued that because administrators must focus on the business and managerial sides of leadership in schools, graduate programs should do the same. In fact, Dembowski's (1998) recommendation is that future administrators acquire an MBA (Master's in Business Administration) to remedy this disparity. Although this advice may resonate for those who know first-hand how challenging it can be to manage school environments and fulfill budgeting responsibilities, this solution probably compromises the more global performance expectations of principals.

This certainly proved to be the case in a study that solicited feedback from early career school leaders and compared the data to the relevant literature (Mullen, 2004). Preliminary findings supported performance of this practicing administrator group in five core leadership areas—school organization, school management, instructional supervision, student services, and community relations. In fact, instructional supervision, not school management, was the area that onsite principals and assistant principals assigned greater priority in their daily and seasonal work. However, this is not to say that technical mentoring approaches to instructional supervision are less prominent for school leaders in their implementation of statewide policies, quality assurance programs, and teacher performance appraisal systems.

Another illustration of technical mentoring takes us to a literature task force from the University of South Florida. In 2002, this faculty team interfaced with a school advisory board of district administrators, including superintendents. This exercise involved obtaining face-to-face feedback on the major domains of leadership capacity (not areas of work as previously described) represented in current educational studies. Through a dialogic process, the faculty wanted to learn about the priorities of administrative decision makers for leadership preparation. Based on the results of the comprehensive review, the faculty identified six responsibilities of site-based leadership: (1) to develop organizational and managerial capacity, (2) to build mentoring systems, (3) to foster collaborative leadership, (4) to promote and practice democracy, (5) to provide ethical leadership, and (6) to foster new ideas of schooling (Mullen, Gordon, Greenlee, & Anderson, 2002, see p. 165).

Not surprisingly, the board members uniformly upheld the importance of the managerial dimension of leadership as a core area of work for schools. They expressed concern that this focus has yet to be translated into the teaching of university faculty within administrator preparation programs. As it turns out, this message is consistent with the persistent call for the integration of theory and practice from educational management theorists (Malone, 2001) and educational leadership theorists (Murphy & Forsyth, 1999). There is a significant array of opinions among academics regarding "technical mentoring." These mostly center on the weight (i.e., heavy or light) that should be attributed by leadership programs to managerial coordination and hence proficiency with **bureaucratic leadership.**

> **Bureaucratic leadership**
> administrative management of an effective and efficient operation within a safe learning environment

The advisory board members explained their unique responsibility for hiring new teachers and administrators directly from university programs and for knowing what it takes to be a successful school leader. From this vantage point, they argued that new principals and assistant principals must have readiness skills in the administrative areas of campus management (e.g., monitoring for safety), financial management (e.g., budgeting), and program management (e.g., scheduling). Interestingly, the ability to effectively manage human relations was "factored into" this leadership capacity and described as a relational value (e.g., embodies a "think 'we,' not 'I,' orientation to others") and informed decision making ("seeks, analyzes, and uses data from a variety of sources") (Mullen, et al., 2002, p. 167).

Similarly, the educational literature is replete with images of technical mentoring that treat relational and human values as areas of managerial concern and competency. While some stress that competency for school leaders necessitates investment in a broader constituency in planning and change, others counter that this very logic has turned public schools into playgrounds for Corporate America, whose political control over the curriculum and manipulation of teachers and children commercializes education in underhanded ways (Steinberg & Kincheloe, 1997b). Social justice advocates warn against such forces of our own making that potentially endanger the "health" of school communities (Riehl, 2000; see also Freire, 1997).

It would be misleading to imply that the Florida-based advisory board under discussion projected value only for technical mentoring. The other five previously identified capacities were also considered integral to balancing the work of mentor leaders and university teaching faculty. However, the skills-based managerial capacity, when seen as an overarching framework, encompasses the mentoring domain: Leaders not only coordinate the daily life of their campuses but also facilitate the technical knowledge required for teacher and student success. Not unlike any leadership behavior, this necessitates a questioning of its underlying assumptions. **Critical democratic mentors** (teachers or leaders) are committed to honest ideological evaluation for the benefit of themselves and others; moreover, their self-reflective subjectivity contends vigorously with cultural, political, social, and historical forces (Kincheloe & Steinberg, 1995).

Such higher education scenarios that have direct relevance for public schools extend into issues of professional and cultural identity. Faculties are currently expected to retool outdated graduate programs and rethink what an "intellectual" is and does in their mentoring role (Nyquist & Woodford, 2000). In education, *intellectual* has been recently translated into **scholar–practitioner leadership** (or leader) (Horn, 2001), which one would assume would be yoked with critical thinking and mentoring as sources of empowerment. However, in practice, scholar–practitioners vary in theoretical insight and convictions. Keeping the reality of variance in mind, scholar–practitioners who facilitate technical mentoring would represent the noncritical end of this spectrum, while those engaged in alternative mentoring would uphold its critical and radical forms (Horn, 2002).

In a teaching study based on a master's class, a group of inservice teachers and administrators was invited to put

> **Critical democratic mentors**
> understand their own ideologies, values, and allegiances and reveal the influence of these orientations on their work and relationships

> **Scholar-practitioner leadership**
> use of theory to inform practice, and reflection to empower action, which can range from the uncritical to the critical

these ideas into reflective action and describe "dynamic scholar practitioner" (Mullen, 2005). The Florida professionals characterized this as someone who is an active learner, proficient at understanding different types of information, including research and technical sources, and who has a profound awareness of the personal self. In addition, the scholar–practitioner was described as a "threefold researcher–practitioner person," but not necessarily as a critical or radical thinker, whose engagement in such leadership activity as data gathering, evaluation, and self-reflection was, once again, thorough. The educators debated seeing themselves as authentic scholar–practitioner leaders or developing public intellectuals. As described, many hesitated, having internalized the constant negativity from external forces, particularly policy-makers, the public, and the media to the effect that educators must be externally controlled because they lack credibility as competent, knowing professionals.

Connections to School Reform

The weight placed on technical standards of responsibility for the nation's schools has turned on the accountability engine to full throttle. Legislative changes and policy reform, combined with public and corporate pressure, have shifted school systems into behaviors akin to technical mentoring: Curriculum alignment with standardized testing materials and the vigilant record-keeping of test scores and associated variables, such as student attendance, have brought managerial coordination squarely to the fore as a primary preoccupation. In this primer, the capacity building of mentoring systems within and across organizations requires **ministerial competency**. In contrast, technocratic mandates necessitate a corresponding focus on managerial competency; this emphasis can even overshadow ministerial competency (Sergiovanni, 1998).

Capitalist practices associated with efficiency, production, and competition have taken the technocratic form of high-stakes testing policies for schools, fueling controversy. For some, the increased standards for student

Ministerial competency
a concern with human relationships, communities, rights, and the common good as well as equity, democracy, and social justice

achievement and accountability to outcome-based performance for teachers have benefited classroom learning, but many believe that K–12 American public schools have come into the limelight for the wrong reasons and for using the wrong tools. Measurable progress is being demanded on both student test scores and school grades, and the results are publicized, comparing disadvantaged schools of low socioeconomic standing to their privileged counterparts. The assumption is that students learn when teachers and schools are held to rigorous standards of accountability and that high-stakes testing is the key to success.

However, citing national testing data from 17 American states, Berliner has demonstrated the radical position that it is "indeterminate" whether increased scores can even be equated with student learning: "While a state's high-stakes test may show increased scores, there is little support in these data that such increases are anything but the result of test preparation and/or the exclusion of students from the testing process" (Amrein & Berliner, 2002, p. 1). Yet these 17 states have also made the high school diploma contingent on an exit test (or final course exams) (Parkay & Stanford, 2004). Politically affiliated companies design these and other statewide school tests, in addition to related tools for test data summary and analysis, accompanying software for test preparation and more, in their suspect role as profiteers, or, to put it critically, grand masters (see, e.g., Ignite! a Texas-based, for-profit company that provides software to Floridian students taking standardized tests, http://www.ignitelearning.com/company.shtml, 2004).

The higher the stakes of a test for schools, the more attention is diverted to test preparation, along with the subjects that incite "red alerts," particularly reading, writing, and math. High-stakes testing policies have incurred a number of costs for principals and teachers caught up in what Grogan (2004) calls a "metanarrative of accountability." She explains that "dumbing down the curriculum" in pursuit of higher test results has led to such problems as cheating, not only by students but also by teachers and school leaders (Amrein & Berliner, 2002). As testimonial data confirm (Bruner & Livingston, 2002), some teachers have students work on test preparation materials in lieu of subject matter content and even turn worksheets into "test formats." Importantly, the issue of political pressure and ethics is correlative in this context—school personnel who succumb to the pressures, fearful of the punitive measures for their schools that fail to make the grade, are probably fearful of the consequences, whether imagined or real.

Such curricular debasements are at least partly fueled by the anxiety felt by practitioners who believe that their school's failing grade could lead to its being, euphemistically speaking, "reconstituted," along with the neighborhoods in which their schools are located (Grogan, 2004). The fear lives on for those schools that have been informed they have just *one* more chance to raise their overall test scores before sweeping penalties are enforced but to what extent is difficult to gauge at this time. Across the nation we continue to hear reports of schools nearly or even actually closed down for failing to meet the acceptable performance standards (Parkay & Stanford, 2004), which may or may not be reflective of a more "global" threat against public school education.

Obviously a state's curriculum standards or frameworks are intended for guiding and delivering instruction, not for teaching students how to take a test. In Arizona, for example, the Arizona Academic Standards are inextricably linked in their conceptualization to the professional development and community of teachers; ongoing dialogue is to be encouraged about the standards and relevant applications to classroom curriculum, particularly in those subjects tested (Arizona Education Association, 2003). And in Florida, it is also expected that the benchmarks will be clearly reflected in various subjects and the assessments developed; to this end, teacher mentors have a role to play in helping to ensure that all teachers have a complete grasp of the Sunshine State Standards (Florida Department of Education, 2003). But the instructional testing milieu across all states has clearly been tied to rewards and penalties for both human beings and institutions, which separates intent from consequence. Even faculty development and mentoring advocates may feel pressured to protect against unknown consequences (and hence inadvertently reinforce the status quo). However, "dumbing down the curriculum" can jeopardize self-efficacy, student learning, and authentic assessment.

Over time we might expect school culture itself to become less rich and multi-faceted if high-stakes standardized testing continues as the primary educational goal to the exclusion of all others except where these provide the necessary support. High quality teaching and training at both the intern and inservice professional stages are two such examples. The morale, reputation, reward structure, and graduation rates of schools have been significantly altered. Increasingly, schools, states, and countries live under the rule of national auditing agencies, notoriously epitomized by the British Office for Standards in English (OFSTED, www.ofsted.gov.uk, 2004), and its vigilant inspections of all schools in England (Scott & Dinham, 2002), which extend to local education authorities and teacher training institutions. The overlapping missions of the Department for Education and Skills (DfES, www.dfes.gov.uk, 2004) and the Teacher Training Agency (TTA, www.tta.gov.uk, 2004) strengthen the OFSTED's influence over the United Kingdom itself.

Relevant to this picture, Tharp and Gallimore (1995/1988) believe that "'technical efficiency'" undermines comprehensive school change and perpetuates life as it is, not as it can be. In their own words: "That schools have not already been reformed testifies to the controlling power of the meaning of 'school' and the necessity to change that meaning" (p. 272). This powerful analysis should make us wonder about whether a broad and deep force exists to preserve traditional and possibly nostalgic meanings of schooling and simultaneously to resist even hopeful systemic changes, a viewpoint that delivers the "choke-point" in this picture.

Beyond Technical Mentoring

While the domination of a technical–rational curriculum for our nation's schools generates negative synergy, it also creates space for democratic mentor leaders to intervene and introduce desirable change. Although high-stakes testing reforms are "focused on eliminating social injustice, with the hopes of increasing the academic achievement of all children," they "fail to identify the dilemmas that are created by models and notions of leadership that are grounded in power-over conceptions" (Brunner, 2002, p. 705). As a poignant example, the *No Child Left Behind Act of 2001* was designed to "force" educational leaders and teachers nationwide to confront the disparities in student achievement for ethnic minority groups; however, most schools in need have not had the necessary external support and resources to remedy the gaps for disadvantaged student groups by, for example, placing a highly qualified teacher in every classroom (Futrell, 2003).

Paradoxically, high-stakes testing turns schools into a survivalist culture. The "de facto" tracking of racial minorities, language-limited learners, and students with special needs and disabilities consequently becomes more prevalent. Further, some school administrations experiencing an undue amount of pressure from high-stakes testing have been caught manipulating test conditions and data (Amrein & Berliner, 2002; Bruner & Livingston, 2002). As reported in local newspapers, certain blocks of students considered a risk to overall scores have been discouraged from being at school on testing days.

As a related force, tracking, in the usual sense of providing a different curriculum, schedule, and teaching staff to particular groups of students, continues. A disproportionate number of African Americans, Latinos, and poor students have typically been segregated in trade and industrial vocational tracks, while mostly white and Asian students are directed into academic tracks. Notably, ability groupings differentiate among students and provide different educational opportunities (Kincheloe, 1999; Oakes, Selvin, Karoly, & Guiton, 1992). Critical scholars (e.g., Joe Kincheloe, Jonathan Kozol, and Jeanne Oakes) believe that "democracy itself will struggle to survive in such circumstances" (Kincheloe, 1995, p. 41).

Such technocratic environments resemble class-based workplaces headed by mentors—not always visible—exercising managerial authority. In contrast, "critical citizens" (Giroux, 1996) or "authentic mentors" (Freire, 1997) would attempt to take full advantage of political and other forms of unity while supporting difference. Demonstrating an "ethic of risk" would, encourages Giroux (1996), summon courage. Such efforts have the potential to expose racism and its transmutations and to keep vigil over the ways in which social forms actually alter and even dampen the democratic impulse of people. From this point of view, how mentors respond to and, moreover, contribute to the changing policy context is essential for creating liberatory mentoring environments that uphold the principles of civil freedom, human rights, and social justice.

Radical curriculum thinkers and historians alike believe that the creative democracy John Dewey envisioned in the early part of the 20th century is highly relevant to this constructivist context. McLaren (1994, 2001) encourages a reframing of the federal government's continuing retreat from social justice in America against a larger historic backdrop. We can apply Dewey's (1916/1997) democratic outlook to the educational issues discussed herein. By doing so, we can see that there is politically different thinking and mentorship associated with the frameworks of "training for occupations" (technical mentoring) and "education through occupations" (alternative mentoring) (Mullen with Kohan, 2002). The Deweyian vision of "education through occupations" offers a means for unifying academic disciplines and vocational curriculum for all students and at the whole school level (see also Dewey's lectures, edited by Clopton & Ou, 1973). The purpose of education organized through occupation rather than through training for industry is to prepare individuals to fully participate in, lead, and even transform society (Kincheloe, 2004a). In a democratic society, students select their own occupations while cultivating the ability to do so.

Ongoing curricular splits in academics and vocations that promote a double standard for traditionally disenfranchised groups have been tolerated by the best of leaders. Critical mentors who are part of a system that models "education through occupations" would, for example, emphasize the fostering of cultural knowledge in relation to self, the infusion of one content area into another, and versatility rather than overspecialization. Such emancipation necessitates reflective, critical thought and action through a system-wide exploration of value structures, reciprocal learning among teachers, interdisciplinary collaboration, and cross-cultural mentoring for groups and institutions as well as other forms of mentorship.

This model of education through occupations is *not* to be misinterpreted as or equated with industrial or vocational education. To build a curriculum around vocational education and on the learning of such skills as cooking and engine repair without the vital context of the social occupations would be to recreate the very schism that privileges academic learning. Importantly, this notion of learning through the occupations is fundamentally aligned with Dewey's belief that educators must prepare the next generation to challenge the status quo. Citizens who are "educated" to operate efficiently in the existing social order are, from this perspective, being trained as subservient workers that obey authority—a manifestation of the hidden curriculum of schooling systems that tacitly regulate learning and behavior within stratified systems of labor (McLaren, 1994; Pinar, et al., 1995/1996). Dewey warns that ability tracking—referred to by him as *vocational education*—is a trap. It perpetuates dangerous beliefs, namely that certain groups should perform particular jobs and that educators should mindlessly adopt standards from business and industry (see Clopton & Ou, 1973).

A curriculum shaped for integrated, holistic learning would, Dewey (1916/1997) contends, create well-rounded individuals rather than potential workers tracked for utility and conformity to existing culture. These students would also be instructed in multiple bodies of knowledge (e.g., economics, civics, and politics) and have the intel-

ligence and motivation for adapting to change. Societies rooted in such constructivist, learner-centered worldviews can foster multiple possibilities for mending the curricular schisms that perpetuate barriers between people and cultures. Political agendas, efficiency standards, and technical mentoring are a combustible mix that produces such oddities as "supervisory mentors," "managerial leaders," and "reactive teachers."

Finally, in order to get beyond technical mentoring and technocratic, antidemocratic mindsets, we would need to "politicize" this Deweyian portrait of an alternative world and bring to the surface its assumptions and limitations. For, as Freire (1997) reminds us, the process of schooling is far too complex to compress the possibilities imagined into a single worldview. In the present context, a pro-Dewey or anti-Dewey position blindly accepted would, ironically, have the potential to reproduce the "power-over conceptions" of socialization and education that we are trying to escape.

Humanitarianism in this context means refusing to turn students and teachers into technically and scientifically trained workers. Authentic mentor leaders search for ways to honor human potential by discovering possibilities not hampered by conformity to, for example, procedural knowledge and guidelines for action (Freire, 1997). The next chapter continues this line of thinking: It sends the hopeful message that our technocratic mentoring worlds can transform through imagination, willpower, and action—together envisioned as significant emancipatory undertakings. This ideal is anchored in real-life examples that draw upon the attributes of learning communities and egalitarian-based relationships. As next discussed, these are just two of the many counterbalances or alternatives available for this democratic purpose.

Glossary

Bureaucratic leadership—administrative management of an effective and efficient operation within a safe learning environment

Critical democratic mentors—understand their own ideologies, values, and allegiances and reveal the influence of these orientations on their work and relationships

Learner-centered mentoring paradigm—a worldview of mentor–mentee relationships grounded in shared discovery and learning, with mentors cast as facilitator or partner

Mentor-driven paradigm—a traditional standard for authoritarian relationships that assume a one-way knowledge conduit and the mentee's passivity, obedience, and mastery of learning

Ministerial competency—a concern with human relationships, communities, rights, and the common good as well as equity, democracy, and social justice

No Child Left Behind Act of 2001—one of the most comprehensive acts pertaining to education, this federal law (signed by President George Bush in 2002) underscored four principles and goals: stronger accountability from schools for results, greater freedom for states and communities, support for research-based educational methods, and more schooling choices for parents

Positivism—scientific linear models that promote technical approaches to mentoring and standards and that discourage importance of context and transformation; perpetuates the belief that human destiny is inevitable

Scholar–practitioner leadership—use of theory to inform practice, and reflection to empower action, which can range from the uncritical to the critical

Questions for Discussion

1. Compare two or more curriculum standards (frameworks) in the states of your choice (in this chapter Arizona, Florida, and North Carolina are all mentioned), and analyze these for insight into technical mentoring (and possibly alternative mentoring) as related to issues of curriculum and assessment. Apply the lessons learned from this chapter.
2. Reflect on the textbooks (or other sources) that you encounter, specifically coursework. Do you believe that intellectually demanding texts can be combined with first-hand, how-to accounts to promote critical thought, or do you think that conflicting ideological frameworks should not be reflected in the selection of texts?
3. Define "critical mentor" and then select someone from the past or present who characterizes this. Brainstorm qualities associated with that individual (e.g., patient listening; philosophical questioning; provocative speaking or writing style) and circle the qualities you are particularly drawn to. Beside each circle, record an example of your

attempt to develop personally (e.g., practice patient listening with peers; ask open-ended questions of self and others; deepen thoughts through draft writing). Now count the circled words. Is the overall number small or large relative to the list itself? Next, search for a possible pattern among the examples of the qualities. To what extent, if any, have you (perhaps unconsciously) identified with another? As a greater extreme, have you been emulating another? After gaining insight into your own unconscious needs and desires as a learner, record your results and then compare them with a friend's.

4. What strengths and drawbacks do you believe might exist for the Deweyian model of academic–vocational integration ("education through occupations") for the school (or institution) in which you intern or are employed? After reflecting on the potential of this model for the setting that is familiar to you, describe your response in words (written or orally). (For additional information about Dewey's educational framework, the relevant sources cited in this chapter can be consulted.)

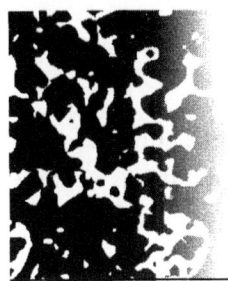

CHAPTER FOUR

Alternative Mentoring

In contrast with technical, or functionalist, mentoring, where the emphasis is on maintaining the status quo through hierarchically entrenched power structures and efficiency frameworks, "alternative mentoring" can be thought of as a contemporary concept. As explained in chapter 2, alternative and radical ideas of mentoring are critical of the technical mentoring agenda. In education, countercultural theories and practices resist mainstream notions of and approaches to teaching and learning as well as research and inquiry. This chapter builds on the "Mentoring and Relationship" section from the Introduction, extends chapter 2's social justice themes, and complements technical mentoring in chapter 3.

New Mentoring Developments

The alternative mentoring literature does not conform to a single "best" framework or form of development, nor does it ascribe to a "one-type-fits-all" solution. Instead, the "best practices" vary from one context to another, and they are influenced by organizational and cultural forces, as well as the aspirations, purposes, and needs of those involved (Allen & Finkelstein, 2003; Darwin, 2000; Freire, 1997).

Mentoring practices specific to school and university contexts have had positive (and mixed) results for groups and, where applicable, dyads. These modes include cohort mentoring, cross-cultural mentoring, peer coaching, school–university partnerships, and telementoring or e-mentoring, to name a few. Each form ideally contributes new stances for remedying the perceived drawbacks of traditional mentoring and offers expanded possibilities for contemporary relationships and structures. Additionally, these methods theoretically support the democratic goal of the equality of all educators' access to professional development opportunities as well as high-quality teacher performance, reciprocal mentoring, and student learning.

Alternative Mentoring Frameworks and Processes

New and expanded ideas of mentorship have emerged from research in undergraduate and graduate classrooms as well as in schools, school–university collaboratives, and community partnerships. Mentoring frameworks and forms conducive to the group structure are of particular interest here, as this emphasis reflects **postmodern** trends in the field. Additionally, the group structure can offer viable solutions to the isolation and abandonment of traditional dyadic arrangements (Horn, 2001) and the lack of community support (Nyquist & Woodford, 2000).

Postmodern
a worldview that confronts metanarratives of truth, stasis, and universal reason and promotes critique, reflection, and empathy

The new forms of mentoring draw upon cognitive psychology, specifically stage and learning theory (Tharp & Gallimore, 1995/1988), which some educators find helpful for clarifying the needs of mentees. Others, however, would counter that such positivist constructs promote simplicity in perspective and paternalism in mentoring relationships. In conflict with this general viewpoint is the ongoing influence of feminist thinking in professional mentoring relationships. The sheer influx of women in the professions over the last several decades, combined with the perspectives they bring, are challenging organizations to change (Christiansen & Ramadevi, 2002; Smith & Smits, 1994). However, far less influence is conspicuous at the levels of executive leadership because of the poor representation of women and minorities in these roles (Banks, 2000).

Mentoring frameworks and processes that have advanced partnerships, particularly team and community learning, can be condensed into six major concepts:

1   comentoring or collaborative mentoring
2   lifelong mentoring
3   sociocultural learning activity
4   mentoring mosaic
5   mentoring (learning) community
6   mentoring leadership or partnership

The following sections discuss the details of these mentoring concepts and explain their tangible application to specific types of groups.

Comentoring or Collaborative Mentoring

Comentoring (Bona, Rinehart, & Volbrecht, 1995) and its spin-offs, *collaborative mentoring* (Mullen, 2000) and *synergistic comentoring* (Mullen & Lick, 1999), are potentially powerful approaches to the human dynamics and learning accomplishments of groups of two or more people. The comentoring or collaborative structure of learning focuses on mutuality and the value of interdependent, reciprocal learning that challenges assumptions about hierarchy, rank, and status—and, consequently, who is "teaching" and who is "learning." This relational or feminist perspective also seeks to promote diversity by bringing together women, minorities, and other traditionally disadvantaged groups.

One mentor–mentee team conducted a self-study of mentoring dyads in literacy education. The students and professors together concluded that the seemingly conflicting roles of mentor and friend could, in fact, be complementary. The concept of mentorship was subsequently seen as *professional friendship*, overcoming the paternalism connoted in the former but without relinquishing the possibility of "being a friend and a mentor at the same time" (Young, Alvermann, Kaste, Henderson, & Many, 2004, p. 23).

Mentoring processes from within dyads and groups interfacing with macrostructures have been deconstructed along lines of authority, power, and oppression, which induces a feminist critique (Beyene, Anglin, Sanchez, & Ballou, 2002; Mullen & Lick, 1999). Mentoring from this critical, self-reflective stance accomplishes two tasks: It promotes social justice agendas, and it enhances learning through synergistic comentoring, an action that affirms both unity and difference in relation to racial, ethnic, and sexual identifications (Sloan & Sears, 2001).

Also, because comentoring can act as a catalyst for bridging theory and practice, cultures of mentoring can be formed and reformed. In one such view of mentoring, "university faculty are [seen as] grounded in theory, while school faculty are grounded in practice, but neither group has established a process with which to mentor one another." A solution is to "enroll both groups to serve as mentors for one another" (Mullen, 2000, p. 5). This type of collaborative comentoring framework can assist professional learning partners by re-examining relationships between educational theory and practice. Comentoring can infiltrate and reshape the socialization process in leadership, teacher development, and higher education and can even rework organizational cultures.

Perhaps the most widely known form of comentoring is **peer coaching** (Danielson & McGreal, 2000; Gottesman, 2000). Although peer coaching is typically considered a mutual, nonevaluative relationship that two experienced teachers share (Portner, 1998), faculty groups also engage at this level but under the umbrella of "self-improvement team" and "learning community."

Applied to the support group context, comentoring can help members cope with and transcend issues often attributed to one-to-one mentoring. For example, school practitioner groups exhibiting a range in learning expertise can exceed what an individual or pair can accomplish (Mullen & Lick, 1999; Mullen, 2005). However, the

---

Peer coaching
a collegial learning process whereby educators assist other experienced faculty in a reciprocal exchange

important but unresolved issue of constructing mentor pairing with respect to gender, ethnicity, age, and discipline (Wilson, Pereira, & Valentine, 2002) is greatly diminished when groups are intentionally diversified and knowledge acquisition is shared by the membership. For instance, women university students generally prefer female mentors, those with whom they can best relate (Wilson et al., 2002). Interestingly, though, a major benefit reported by many women with white male mentors is a familiarity with the long-established, coveted power structures that impact academic and career success.

Lifelong Mentoring

Lifelong learning refers to the self-actualization of individuals as learners and to their embarking on "a lifelong course of learning" (Herman & Mandell, 2004, p. 1). Mentoring and lifelong learning can be seen as closely related processes, as the latter reflects the developmental and sociocultural context of mentorship: "The lifelong capacity of humans to form affectively strong relationships, broadly analogous to attachment/bonding processes of early infancy, is a foundational requirement for mentoring to occur" (Gallimore et al., 1992, p. 6).

These ideas lead us to ask, how does lifelong mentoring translate into the personal practical experience of individuals? A "cartoonish" notion, one may feel struck by the impossibility of the mentor or mentee shadowing the other throughout an entire lifetime (Mullen & Kealy, 1999). Voltaire's (1956) *Candide* is a parody of this level of commitment. Candide, the student, was mentored by Pangloss, the philosopher–optimist, through a series of major disasters (e.g., earthquakes) and tragedies (e.g., flogging) only to conclude, after years of momentous hardship that never turned into anything worthwhile, that the mentoring journey must be lifelong. However, mentoring for life does *not* imply or entail an extended one-on-one mentoring relationship against all odds. Rather, it suggests an ongoing commitment to seek opportunities for mentoring and being mentored as well as for learning and sharing the value of one's experiences.

Mentors, identified as lifelong learners, attempt to learn the art of mentoring by practicing it with their students and others and by doing so within a governing context that they integrate into the work or inquiry at hand: "As scholars, they become more and more expert in the contents of their fields. As teachers, they learn to be more eloquent and deft [at encouraging students to become] active and increasingly independent learners" (Herman & Mandell, 2004, p. 141). Instructors, academic supervisors, or mentors can assist their students, whether at the undergraduate or graduate level, in developing a robust mentoring identity as practitioner, researcher, and activist. Importantly, the mentor can display the potential for learning as a coach and a collaborator and for evoking in the mentee the potential to function as a guide. Protégés can also be taught to take responsibility for initiating agendas and projects and to facilitate the mentor's own learning. Lifelong mentoring practices thereby aid in the sharing of power and knowledge between and among those who strive to expand their identities and effectiveness as colearners and comentors.

While mentoring shares common ground with teaching, it can be distinguished in some very crucial ways. Mentoring and teaching are not interchangeable concepts in theory, and the actions of mentors and teachers can sometimes differ. Notably, classroom teachers can certainly function as mentors to particular students or to novice educators; for example, they are not considered "mentors" to their students except under extraordinary circumstances. Second, mentors rise to the occasion of engaging in mentoring activity. This requires personal time and energy in order to assist learners or colleagues and depends on their "going above and beyond" as educators—even where incentive programs and other reward structures are lacking. Third, mentors value shared and even collaborative work with their students, helping their students become skilled and oriented as "lifelong independent learners." By framing reflective dialogues that promote learning, mentors help protégés to think more deeply; they ask such open-ended questions as "what do you want to learn?" "how might you go about investigating your questions?," and "what contribution do you want to make to the world?" Mentors, like teachers, address their students' practical needs, but they also help "each one and one at a time" to "conceive and complete an academic education that responds to . . . practical and contemplative needs" (Herman & Mandell, 2004, p. 2). Finally, mentors assume a political role when they engage their organizations in becoming genuine learning communities committed to student-and-faculty development and success.

Lifelong learning is also relevant to the protégé's journey itself. As Clark, Harden, and Johnson (2000) discuss, "graduate students who successfully secure mentors appear to be proactive in seeking such relationships" (p. 264), regardless of their school discipline or career goals. This statement also pertains to undergraduate students and employees more broadly. Proactive mentees tend to have a higher overall success rate—they complete their programs, receive solid evaluations, obtain job placement, and, not least, become mentors to others (Dorn & Papalewis, 1997).

Importantly, the exemplary protégé reaches out and assumes leadership in a number of ways. This individual makes contact with faculty as well as former and current students, observes the characteristics of faculty and their actions, pursues developing dyads and/or joining groups, and conducts research to make informed judgments, not only about personally relevant program decisions but also about mentoring choices. These mentees accomplish these and other major steps as well-organized, persistent planners who develop an appreciation of authentic mentoring and, in turn, model this for others (for a fuller description of these phases relative to graduate students, see Johnson & Huwe, 2003, p. 80).

Finally, the concept of lifelong learning has been nationally codified as a standard of professional teaching excellence. For example, this idea that may strike some readers as elusive or indeterminate has been explicitly tied to National Board Certification. The National Board for

Professional Teaching Standards (NBPTS)—an independent, nonprofit, nongovernmental organization created in 1987 in response to *A Nation at Risk* and *A Nation Prepared*—has certified "accomplished teaching" contingent upon demonstration of lifelong learning and teacher mentoring (www.nbpts.org, 2004). Board-certified teachers, as well as mentor teacher candidates seeking NBPTS certification—which some school districts mandate (as a form of compulsory mentoring in return for having covered most of the cost of certification)—are expected to function as "learning coaches" inside and outside the classroom. By mentoring new teachers, it is anticipated that NBPTS teachers will function as change agents, helping to decrease the high attrition rate of teachers while advocating for professional development and overall teacher quality.

Sociocultural Learning Activity

Sociocultural learning conditions must be accounted for when creating activities for fostering and sustaining mentoring. Dewey (1938) illuminates the value of "activity settings" for educators as they attempt to promote "experiences that lead to growth" (pp. 39, 40). Tharp and Gallimore's (1995/1988) notion of *activity setting* highlights human activity, context, and time as integral to education, and the role of pedagogues in changing contexts to affect activity and development (see also Gallimore et al., 1992). This concept blends tenets from several disciplines, with a stake in educational theory and, specifically, Vygotsky's psychological theories of learning and instruction. These researchers purport that all human activity takes place in specific contexts; to change human activities, teachers must study the contexts that drive the activities.

The hypothesis of activity setting as integral to student learning and teacher effectiveness was applied at the grassroots level to the Kamehameha Early Education Project. Based upon the premises of "sociocultural learning activity" and joint productivity, Tharp and Gallimore's (1995/1988) interdisciplinary, "multimethodological" public school literacy program focused on the "development of cognitive/linguistic abilities" (p. 122). Peer coaching techniques were combined with teacher–student instructional conversation and role modeling to assist at-risk ethnic minority native Hawaiian children to develop through reading, talking, and speaking. The activity setting itself took the form of independent stations, such as the listening-skills center, designed to harness peer learning among students and assistance from teachers. The success of this program prompted similar school-based efforts with other marginalized ethnic groups, including Latino Americans in Los Angeles and Native Americans on a Navajo reservation in Arizona.

Many inspired spin-offs have since occurred, including a school-based project undertaken in Haifa, Israel. Herein, the Teachers' Peer Learning Community program was designed to empower teachers to become "agents of change" through the use of advanced technologies and interdisciplinary curricula. For this sociocultural learning activity that occurred for 12 group sessions, the participants broke past their individual isolation and developed collaborative working teams. They attempted to transfer the new cognitive learning and mentoring skills from one environment to another—their own classroom (Almog & Hertz-Lazarowitz, 1999).

Mentoring needs, abilities, and resources are essential to sociocultural mentoring activity. These components are especially effective when integrated and can be used to help identify those aspects of mentoring that best nurture the mentee at a particular time.

Mentoring needs. A person's mentoring needs will vary in accordance with goals and growth patterns. We have greater needs as a student or young person, for example, than as an established professional or adult or even a retiree. Self-concept theorists such as Maslow (1962) refer to an evolution of needs over one's lifetime, from survival and safety concerns to those of social acceptance and self-actualization. The need for productive and satisfactory learning environments, for example, can be used to build self-actualizing mentoring capacity. Constructivist agendas focused on learner-centered curriculum, with the use of cooperative group learning as a key strategy for fostering leadership and citizenry, have been strongly advocated for all student populations, including undergraduate and graduate university programs (Shapiro, 2003). One purpose of support groups, then, is to bring together those with stronger and weaker mentoring self-concepts to create viable and fulfilling contexts.

Mentoring models. These models typically identify primary attributes of a good mentor as role model, nurturer, and caregiver. Anderson and Shannon's (1988) classic work specifies the functions of an ideal mentor: teacher, sponsor, one who encourages, counselor or problem-solver, and friend—one who accepts and relates to the protégé. The mentor and mentee as friends is a theme emphasized by Gallimore and colleagues (1992), who assert that attraction and attachment (i.e., intellectual and interpersonal chemistry) underlie all effective mentorships. Alternative models of professional friendship, emotional intimacy, and authentic communication (Gallimore et al., 1992; Young et al., 2004) support this view.

Mentoring abilities. In contrast to the needs components are one's abilities and their function in determining the appropriate mix of requisite mentoring roles. Abilities of mentors vary with individual characteristics (and combinations) and include, for example, empathy, content specialization, networking capability and connection, goodwill, and social intelligence.

Regarding the abilities of mentors, questions to ask include: what characteristics make a good mentor, and can they be developed? And, how is "success" determined? And for mentees: what is the capacity for self-mentoring or for monitoring one's own progress? To "mentor" one's self is a contradiction in terms, as mentoring depends on an outside source to stimulate, promote, or guide some aspect of learning. However, this particular twist has been gradually integrated into the overall meaning of mentorship.

The teaching portfolio exemplifies this nexus of self-mentoring and mentoring. One such popular form is the

NBPTS school-site portfolio, which shows evidence of teaching practice through student work and knowledge, videotapes of classroom interaction, and written commentaries (www.nbpts.org). However, the focus on teacher reflection, inquiry, and professional development closely links to issues of assessment, review, and promotion, as the NBPTS judges the work for the competitive purposes of certification.

Similarly, the professional development portfolio is nestled within competency-based decision making and certification for preservice teachers. Mirroring the more advanced NBPTS portfolio, it serves as a vehicle for monitoring progress and for promoting reflection and as documented evidence that learning has occurred (Moon & Mayes, 1995). Both of these functions are akin to the mentee's cognitive and creative ability and drive to direct self-development; however, the added dimension of portfolio assessment within the context of the national teaching standards has introduced the paradox of evaluation. As this book reports, a similar conundrum has been seen in the peer coaching context: The pressure that the standards movement has placed on professional accountability for teachers has moved collaborative learning among faculty (i.e., self-and-other mentoring) into the formal assessment domain.

Mentoring resources. Resources for mentoring include time, space, and materials as well as network alliances. Materials might consist of books, computers, self-help guides, and films. Resources in and beyond the protégé's immediate environment involve peers, mentors (e.g., teachers and advisors), administrators, and staff (relational), as well as workshops, conferences, electronic databases, and grants (nonrelational). Contexts providing mentoring resources broadly encompass college, school, family, and church (Allen & Finkelstein, 2003).

Mentoring Mosaic

Depending upon an individual's needs, **mentoring mosaics** enable access to multiple figures for learning,

Mentoring mosaic
a collegial network of multiple mentors and opportunities for growth

feedback, and support. Mosaics can be created as a primary or secondary network or as a more informal resource. Mosaics are amorphous in the sense that while they have originated with a specified name and for a particular purpose, they assume various guises, such as "network," "community," "family," and even "resource." Mentoring mosaics play a practical, if not essential, role in helping protégés optimize the effects of mentoring. In fact, Head, Reiman, and Thies-Sprinthall (1992) strongly encourage mentees to access such a network of secondary mentors for addressing shortcomings in the primary mentor–mentee dyad. Mentees should consider participating in mosaics to expand academic and career opportunities. They also ward off disappointment as actors reaching out beyond dyadic arrangements, as mentors cannot be "everything" to any one person.

Another interpretation of mentoring mosaic is as a "relationship constellation," proposed by Kram (1985/1988) as a strategy for providing career development support to anyone encountering barriers in the workplace. Over the last 20 years Kram's groundbreaking studies in mentoring and equity have inspired many researchers to seek information about structural hurdles faced by women and minorities in both work and academic contexts (Smit, 2003). Regarding its use in practice, the mosaic notion has been applied to various populations and contexts, including a school–university collaborative seeking robust alternatives to ineffectual systems (Mullen & Lick, 1999).

Within the mentoring mosaic, the individual taps the strengths and qualities of one's partners. Members interchange roles as mentors and protégés, sponsoring the learning of all parties through a synergistic, flexible structure. This kind of network is indispensable for cultivating peer mentors; compensating for the dissatisfactions of traditional mentoring relations; and facilitating larger, team-oriented projects (Mullen & Kealy, 1999).

In *Piano Lessons*, radio talk show host Noah Adams (Adams, 1996) chronicles his odyssey, at age 50, of learning to play the piano, which includes having resisted advice to take formal lessons from a piano teacher. In the end, ironically, the need for beginners to learn from teachers becomes one of the author's deepest realizations and major recommendations. This autobiography demonstrates the creation of a mentoring mosaic in a professional's life. What Adams created was a musical mentoring mosaic that brought together all of these resources and his own needs and abilities. Among those whom Adams describes as having had a powerful impact on his goal to play piano are such role models as famous piano players Glen Gould and Jellyroll Morton. Also included are people who know about the instrument itself and who represent the lore of piano playing and piano making. And then there are inspiring teachers. In Adams's case, a family, consisting entirely of teachers, perhaps best captures the metaphor of mentoring mosaic: In a single home, every room had a piano that linked the harmony of one with many.

Indeed, if mentoring is defined more as a process than an activity performed by an individual, then several people can simultaneously perform the traditional roles of mentoring (e.g., nurturing, advising, befriending, instructing). Importantly, this constitutes a decentralization of traditional mentorship and power-based relationships into power-sharing arenas. Within such a network, one person may serve as a subject specialist, another as counselor, and still others as advocate, advisor, and promoter. Regarding the Neo-Impressionist movement, for example, Seurat was its "source" or originator; Dubois-Pillet was the movement's organizer; and Signac and Fénéon were promoters of the group's artistic ideas.

The mosaic framework is a significant strategy for arts-based communities and universities, and, importantly, for schools and other organizations. Hargreaves and Fullan (2000) believe that mentoring mosaics should involve not just one-on-one contact but rather a whole-school culture engaged in "reculturing" itself. Such school-based mentoring can support the growth of beginning teachers through a process of team-building. Herein, multiple mentors offer numerous resources and ways of learning.

Mentoring mosaics, however, are not necessarily inclusive and socially transformative. In fact, they can be elitist, even within our own public schools built upon the premise of democracy. Based on her first-hand knowledge of a wide range of learners, a Spanish teacher revealed that "mentoring in the secondary context is not even available to all students." About this serious omission, she reflects that many students

> neither qualify for special assistance nor are assigned advisors. . . . Possibly these students lack the skills needed to relate with adults comfortably enough to form alliances across status differences. Perhaps they are unable to find a suitable mentor, especially if they are minority students and/or female. Some of these students may establish a peer-support system, or a "mentoring mosaic," but others may be unable to. (Mullen & Lick, 1999, p. 145)

Assuming that mentoring is essential to academic success, Merriam (1983) reinforces that "what mentoring is, who will be a mentor, and who is to receive mentoring should be more clearly defined" (p. 145).

Mentoring (Learning) Community

Mentoring (learning) community
formal or informal arrangements that bring together any combination of scholars, practitioners, students, stakeholders, and activists to inquire into practice and promote professional development

Mentoring communities have different names, take different forms, and perform different functions. They have existed in the professions and in education for a long time (Christiansen & Ramadevi, 2002) yet remain somewhat indefinable, largely due to the countless ways in which they can be conceptualized and shaped for practice. Such communities can, broadly speaking, sponsor membership for scholars, teachers, leaders, students, activists, stakeholders, or a combination of these. Importantly, Wenger (1998), a learning community scholar, believes that everyone—including mentors and mentees—belongs to one or more communities of practice that are not always labeled. Currently popular are the configurations widely known, even among policymakers, as "professional learning communities" and "communities of practice," with the everyday use of "learning community," "discourse community," "network," and "cohort," among others.

Today, a prevalent concept of education that frames teachers' work is the professional learning community. Some equate this with accountability measures, others with opportunities for learning or renewal. An empirical study involving the site-based transitional experiences of 50 beginning teachers working in Massachusetts public schools focused on the concept of the professional learning community, viewing it as three types: "veteran-oriented professional cultures," "novice-oriented professional cultures," and "integrated professional cultures." In the first instance, it was found that where mentoring programs existed in the schools, the assigned novice teacher–expert teacher relationships were mostly "deeply disappointing." Faring only slightly better, the novice-oriented professional cultures produced another kind of difficulty—while the new teachers quickly became collegial, they also felt lost, as they were receiving inadequate support. In the last instance, where the schools demonstrated integrated professional cultures, the novice teachers experienced successful, reciprocal relationships with veteran teachers and their own colleagues within dynamic systems of support (Kardos, Johnson, Deske, Kauffman, & Liu, 2001).

Also, it is important to recognize that, in the current lexicon of standards, the primary function of the professional learning community is not teacher development, group affinity, and ongoing learning. Instead, this idea of community has been dovetailed with student learning and achievement as the context for professional teacher development and the specific roles of coach and facilitator (DuFour & Eaker, 1998; NBPTS, www.nbpts.org, 2004). As one such example, a teacher-based survey of Philadelphia elementary schools' Children Achieving program confirmed that schools with the highest 4th-grade reading scores had a "greater sense of teacher professional community" (Tighe, Wang, & Foley, 2002).

In Portner's (2001) view, learning communities that are formalized for teachers, and presumably mandated, require four interrelated provisions of support:
- Commitment and participation from key individuals and leaders
- Compatible relationships within the macrosystem in which the mentoring occurs
- A viable structure for developing and implementing

the mentoring effort and assessing and evaluating
- A thorough body of resources (time, funds, staff, material, and equipment)

The teacher knowledge and narrative inquiry paradigms in educational research suggest an idea of teacher community and empowerment that conflicts with the above. Decades of research on communities of school-based practice have emphasized teacher knowledge, biography, and collaboration, as well as the premise that educators need safe places to assemble, work through issues of authority, and actively consider their classrooms as places of ongoing inquiry and themselves as teacher researchers.

This conceptualization of the learning community views learning and sharing as enlivening processes that simply cannot be mandated, since the explicit assumption is that one *chooses* to belong to a learning community. Clandinin and Connelly (e.g., 1992, 1995) construct an additional view of "teacher as curriculum maker," which recognizes the capacity of teachers to empower themselves to function collaboratively, professionally, and independently within a landscape of externally imposed standards and policies.

Attention to the voluntary nature of communities is a new theme in the literature. Related studies portray teacher-to-teacher mentoring communities as sources of collaborative mentorship that heighten teacher awareness, creativity, and self-efficacy through multiple partnerships. In teacher education and leadership studies, the mentoring community has been construed as a faculty–student dyad (Flockhart & Woloshyn, 2001) and as an extended faculty–student network (Diamond & Mullen, 1999a). In the network context in particular, mentors engage in self-study practice and are continually reinventing themselves as comentors and colearners through partnership, meaning-making, dialogue, and action.

Comentoring advocates believe educators such as Freire (1997) and even corporate executives (Duff, 1999) can encourage a process of constant change and renewal, causing educators to re-educate themselves. While each arrangement is different, they are all collaboratively oriented; that is, they model new forms of authority, discourse, and pedagogy or inquiry. Such productive partnerships and arrangements cannot be mandated but must remain free to grow through a negotiated version of comentoring.

As Jaffee (2004) describes, even if such communities are compulsory, as in the case of the learning community for college freshmen, they can nonetheless be centered "on the bonds of friendship, cohesiveness, and unity" (p. B16). However, as will be seen in the "Cohort Mentoring" subsection, learning communities that are required for course credit at any level of the educational system tend to have mixed results. Nonetheless, in most cases the positives seem to outweigh the drawbacks, favoring formalized learning communities for students.

Mentoring Leadership or Partnership

Mentoring leadership
leaders and partners whose creative visions of mentorship help transform organizational relationships and systems

Mentoring leadership (Mullen & Lick, 1999), a proactive form of partnership, has a broad reach in the educational literature. The focus here is on the nexus between mentoring and leadership as related to alternative mentoring, specifically learning communities. Many assume that formally recognized leaders alone make *the* difference in the strongest and healthiest of our organizations. However, Fullan (e.g., 1999) and others believe that this overgeneralization misses the point that synergistic comentoring partners, particularly teachers, shoulder significant change efforts, and effective principals may unduly receive credit for the contributions of entire teams.

Recognizing the invaluable role of formal leadership, some practicing school leaders argue that the principal as lead mentor has a distinctive function. Together with the administrative team, this individual sets the conditions for shared leadership that, in turn, enable teachers, parents, and students to work effectively as partners. In the words of one K–12 public school director, "The degree to which the team is effective is largely determined by the lead mentor's willingness to develop vision, set far-reaching goals, successfully obtain resources, maintain a constructive climate, nurture planned change, and constantly check system processes" (Mullen & Lick, 1999, p. 230).

A related issue is that lead mentors understand that many people "buy into" the myth that organizations have "rigid internal divisions that inhibit inquiry across divisional boundaries" (Senge, 1990, p. 66). Systems thinkers encourage leaders and partners to view their organizations as "living systems," that is, as ecosystems with underlying structures that can be changed (Senge, 1990; Wheatley, 1999). An implication for leaders of schools is that they can benefit from gaining knowledge of how natural systems function and how organizations can be restructured to imitate organic processes that emphasize development, holism, and change. However, natural systems also experience conditions of change, contradiction, and ambiguity, which must be recognized and tolerated in the larger picture.

As change agents on the "ground level," however, principals and other leaders do not expect to manage every decision and to meet with every team engaged in decision making. In fact, they would likely be seen as controlling if they even attempted to do so. They provide mentoring support by delegating responsibility for important work and by encouraging others to assume leadership roles. In other words, they recognize the grassroots value inherent in teacher-led community efforts and focus groups, such as school improvement teams (Mullen with Sullivan, 2002). In turn, faculty-led teams operate on the democratic premise that the lead mentor (and other key stakeholders) is a vital member of the learning organization itself, regardless of whether he or she functions center stage or on the sidelines (DuFour & Eaker, 1998).

Principals considered exemplary within their academically struggling school communities have successfully fostered the abilities of their workers and the capacities of their organizations. Beyond managerial coordinator, they rise to the occasion as a mentor leader who fulfills the functions of instructional leader, organizational builder, community partner, democratic decision-maker, and collaborator. In general, the field of educational administration reinforces these mentoring images of the highly functioning, multitasking leader who builds school capacity (Schmidt, 2002).

There is increasing evidence that partners who take turns leading and following, regardless of their formal role or title, demonstrate mentoring leadership of a high caliber (Mullen, 2004, 2005). In fact, the more synergistically a team functions from the bottom up, the less indispensable will be the formally recognized role of leader and the perceived need for top-down control (Fullan, 1999). This portrait of leadership could be characterized as alternative mentoring, and yet the indication remains strong that lead mentors are the point of convergence for their organizations (Mullen & Graves, 2000). DuFour and Eaker (1998) clarify: "Empowered teachers and strong principals are not mutually exclusive goals. Schools that operate as learning communities will have both" (p. 188). While some might see this as an image of "contemporary" leadership, others would refer to it as power-based, skills-focused technical mentoring.

In fact, the extent to which lead mentors can be fully absorbed into whole-school learning communities remains an open question, as principals are expected to be results-oriented and standards-minded, which can alter the complexion of such groups. Nonetheless, DuFour and Eaker (1998) have chosen to err on the side of believing that schools should construct a holistic image of the professional learning community wherein principals perform such critical functions as promoting shared leadership and governance and joint decision making and ownership of solutions. In a series of case studies, a group of exemplary practicing school administrators (Tom Graves, Eileen McDaniel, Elaine Sullivan, Lynne Patrick, and Glenn Thomas) has expressed outlooks on mentoring leadership and the role of mentor leader that concur with DuFour and Eaker's perspective on the engaged principal (Mullen & Graves, 2000; Mullen & Lick, 1999; Mullen, 2004; Mullen with Sullivan, 2002).

The mentoring leadership or partnership framework depends upon a number of key components, regardless of whether the organizational leadership style is traditional or alternative. One involves bottom-up leadership or democratic partnership, and the other centers on systems thinking, which can be approached democratically or traditionally. Peter Senge's (1990) systems-thinking perspective proposes that principals and other systems leaders develop frameworks for envisioning the whole and specifically "for seeing interrelationships rather than things, for seeing patterns of change rather than static 'snapshots'" (p. 68). Many educators, including former school principal Schmidt (2002), agree that "[good mentors] are big-picture people who can see farther down the road than you ever dreamed of going, and pinpoint the skills you need to get there" (p. 149).

However, as Laurel Wheatley (1999) counters, vision, which provides purpose and direction for an organization, should not be viewed as a destination but rather as a "formative influence." Margaret Wheatley's articulation seems to include more of the role of faculty and others as mentoring partners who share the role of leadership and decision-making vital to an organization's capacity to improve and sustain itself. Leaders work alongside others as team players, and partners rise from deep within the infrastructure of organizations to perform executive leadership tasks.

A final point about mentoring leadership or partnership is the idea that everyone must learn to live with contradiction, and mentors and partners are certainly no exception. Like all professionals, mentor principals and school and university leaders must find creative ways to bridge democracy and accountability. These may seem to be opposing political ideologies in theory, but they are not necessarily always in practice. The concept of democratic accountability grew out of a school study (Mullen & Graves, 2000) and the realization that, for any school or organization, the poles of democracy and accountability coexist. Each undergirds the other, reinforcing the paradox of what it means to lead in a larger context that values freedom *and* responsibility, autonomy *and* standards.

Specific Forms of Mentoring in Action

The support group continues to be a primary form of teaching and learning within schools, universities, and businesses. For the purposes of this chapter, the following six mentoring types will be discussed:

1. support groups
2. study groups
3. cohort mentoring
4. cross-cultural mentoring
5. telementoring or e-mentoring
6. arts-based mentoring

Support Groups

American anthropologist Margaret Mead once said, "Never doubt that a small group of thoughtful, committed citizens can change the world. Indeed, it's the only thing that ever has" (Ruminate this: eQuotes, http://www.ruminatethis.com, 2004). **Support groups** are "transition communities" constituted by "people who want to undergo the same sort of change" and who "depend on one another to help fulfill [similar] needs and solve [similar] problems" (Bruffee, 1999, p. 74).

> **Support group**
> temporary, transitional structures for satisfying human needs and meeting goals, with potential for more established and sustaining forms

It is important to note that the approach taken here does not reflect this "purist" stance. Instead, *support group* can be viewed much more comprehensively as an overarching category in which all mentoring groups (e.g., study groups) function as specific examples or types. At one end of the support group spectrum, such groups reflect a casual or cooperative model of learning. However, while this approach can foster expedient or experimental ends, it can favor the former. This means that the focus will be on satisfying short-term pedagogical goals. As Bruffee (1999) warns, there is a tendency within college classrooms and other transitory groups to slip into the traditional roles of mentor and mentee, hence entrenching students in non-reflective "busy work." At the other end of this spectrum are intentionally formed support groups that experiment seriously with transformations in challenging areas, particularly involving personal cultural identity. As another warning, such wholesale commitments to development can prove disappointing or even dysfunctional where, for example, the act of emulating one's mentor is expected or attempted at the expense of nurturing one's own interests, values, and identity. Further, one must be prepared for individual and shared ideals to fall short of the intended target. High-risk learning ventures can provoke institutional barriers and unforeseen dynamics in human behavior, particularly when manifested by groups (Jaffee, 2004).

Study Groups

Study group
voluntary membership of students, teachers, or other persons gathering informally or formally to accomplish a short- or long-term goal

Study group has been defined as "a small group of school personnel joining together to increase their capacity [willingness and ability] through new learning opportunities for the benefit of students and the school" (Lick, 1999b, p. 203). Study groups—also known as learning groups, collaborative groups, and consortia—include voluntary membership by those with vision, passion, and energy; purpose(s) and strategies emergent from discourse and agreement; and conceptual and concrete group work.

Potential drawbacks of study groups involve lack of credit for the work, time, and energy involved; process and product concerns; individual ego as opposed to the development of a collective identity; and respecting difference and maximizing unity (Connect with Others, http//www.fieldbook.com/study_groups/studygroupsHow; Mullen & Lick, 1999; Mullen, 2000). (For further information on forming study groups and related processes, refer to the entry "Connect with Others" in the "Resources" section.)

Cohort Mentoring

Mentoring cohort
faculty-student support group that brings together learners with an academic instructor(s) or dissertation chair(s)

The **mentoring cohort** model is a precious but insufficiently tapped resource in higher education (Horn, 2001). Both formal and informal cohort mentoring occurs in our institutions, but the institutionalized option is much better documented. Conversely, informal mentoring may involve greater commitment and risk, as the assistance promised to an individual may or may not occur. Informal mentoring is also differentiated from formal mentoring through the greater affinity experienced by the mentor and the mentee, in addition to the greater emphasis placed on interpersonal contact and the longer duration of the relationship itself (Blake-Beard, 2001; Mullen, 2005).

Reflective learning that neither sacrifices the value of scholarship nor the growing demands of the workplace is typically a goal for mentoring cohorts (Horn, 2001). Many doctoral students and some graduate mentoring faculty especially value cohorts that have a dissertation focus. As recognized in the adult education literature, dissertation cohort groups enable supervisors "to simultaneously manage a substantial number of doctoral students" (Witte & James, 1998, p. 54). In terms of advantages to students, such cohorts confront the perennial problem of disillusionment and academic failure as well as writing and inquiry challenges (Dorn & Papalewis, 1997; Horn, 2001).

Undergraduate populations also gain from membership in faculty–student support groups. In order to succeed, most freshmen need transitional assistance. As Bruffee (1999) attests, "The most important tool college and university professors have to help students re-acculturate themselves into the knowledge communities they aspire to join is mobilizing transition communities" (p. 74). Scaffolds for college success include a focus on study group skills and time management, life skills and problem-solving strategies, and personal and family stresses. Universities typically offer at least one course called The Freshman Year Experience (or the equivalent) that deals with such an introductory curriculum (Jaffee, 2004).

This mentoring cohort to which many freshmen belong throughout their entire undergraduate program is a forum in which pedagogical challenges and group dynamics can intensify. Teachers have expressed that these learning communities tend to be unruly and immature. Mentoring groups that have strongly bonded may initially see newcomers, students and faculty alike, as unwanted members or even potential sources of threat (Mullen, 2005). And Jaffee (2004) adds that sociopsychological forces can segregate particular students or undermine teacher authority, as in demands for less work, changes in syllabi, and unfair evaluations.

Cross-Cultural Mentoring

Cross-cultural mentoring embraces community-based mentoring, diversity awareness education, antiracist curriculum, equity and access in schooling, and electronic learning communities. Such mentoring can occur in community-based organizations that are either "indigenous"—inside the community they belong to—or "exogenous," outside the communities they serve, or both. As Jones (1992) further explains, while school–business collaborations have received a great deal of attention, partnerships between schools and other entities, particularly nonprofit organizations, have not. Local community-based centers in which volunteers offer services can function as invaluable systems of support, providing a range of social and educational services.

Two such community-based U.S. programs—Connecting Generations: Intergenerational Initiative and National Mentoring Partnership Today (for details, see the "Resources" section)—are among those that recognize the need to connect longevity with intergenerational mentoring for the benefit of young people, especially those at-risk of academic failure and school dropout. In fact, inner-city schools, especially those populated by academically at-risk, low-income students of color, benefit from the support of a compassionate community.

One such elementary school in Montgomery, Alabama, actively attracts resources, donors, partners, volunteers, and afterschool tutoring and athletic services. Principal Lynne Patrick's process of building capacity within her school relies upon a whole-community effort. Assuming responsibility for developing and sustaining the school's initiatives, the participatory stakeholder groups consist of churches; Strategies to Elevate People (STEP) program (supports public housing residents); community organizations (YMCA), Boys and Girls Club of America (academic tutoring and athletic organization); and health professionals (Mullen, 2004).

Another form of community-based mentoring is the "culture circle." In this context, grassroots activists and other stakeholders gather to explore what is deemed politically necessary, transformative work (Freire, 1997). Within the culture circle, each person's story is understood historically, culturally, and sociopolitically but also personally and interpersonally. Members commit to remaking hierarchical school systems, specific political "causes," and intellectual traditions. The corporate world, too, offers its own version of this forum—the WOW'M Mentoring Circle—for women professionals who participate in "weekend mentoring" in which they share experiences and stories and offer professional advice and assistance (Duff, 1999).

A related philosophy of mentoring cohorts views the building of the community itself as the core activity. Experimental groups position themselves as a collective critically studying itself (Horn, 2001; Mullen, 2005). Horn (2001) sees the value in mentoring cohorts reflecting on the members' diversity in terms of ethnicity, gender, class, age, and perspective, and, presumably, in questioning and changing homogeneous configurations. As such, mentoring cohorts offer a forum for advancing social justice agendas. Through social acts of interdependence, cohorts provide potentially fertile ground for making connections to schools and other organizations, which are channels for consciousness-raising and activism, and for transforming traditional and elitist cultures (Bruffee, 1999).

Telementoring or E-mentoring

Telementoring
computer-based mentoring involving online communications where the mentor, a specialist in a field of interest, provides academic or professional guidance to mentees

Telementoring or e-mentoring has become the pinnacle of technology-driven epistemologies and innovations in education today. Also known as online mentoring and cybermentoring, it takes such popular forms as distance education, web-enhanced (hybrid) learning, and video teleconferencing (Kealy & Mullen, 2003a, p. 5). Such computer-mediated communications are the primary form of contact in this kind of mentoring.

There are several key elements in fostering learning conditions for groups in an online environment. Covered in greater detail in Kealy and Mullen (2003a) are the following three premises that the telementoring literature describes for successful electronic learning communities:

- *Systematizing mentoring:* The educational experience must be systematically developed through structured activity, which contrasts with the assumption that mentoring will spontaneously occur in the online context. Packard, Walsh, and Seidenberg (2004) argue that female college students and other disadvantaged groups benefit from electronic modalities that encourage adaptation and learning through a structured discourse community (chat rooms and threaded conversation are especially valued).
- *Diversifying mentoring:* Technology users must mentor support groups in education (e.g., preservice teachers, prospective administrators) about diversity more broadly and in ways supportive of infiltrating male-dominated (academic and career) domains, particularly engineering and science (Kasprisin, Single, Single, & Muller, 2003). Examples include new course methods (e.g., two-way videoconferencing) used in teacher education programs wherein white, middle-class student interns gain exposure to diverse populations and increased awareness about diversity as well as pedagogical issues facing urban schools.
- *Humanizing mentoring:* Regardless of the instructional medium selected (e.g., distance learning and hybrid learning), all student populations can potentially benefit from online personal communication with peers and faculty, which also extends to the counseling aspects of mentoring. Regardless of the selected instructional medium, high-quality interaction in educational relationships continues to be regarded as indispensable (Mullen, 2005). At Open University in the United Kingdom, for example, electronic cafes are places where peers connect and do work. Such creative methods have been implemented to help socialize students to the new challenges of mentoring and learning (Kealy & Mullen, 2003a).

Arts-Based Mentoring

Arts-based mentoring is a new term used to describe the role of the arts in creating and furthering acts of mentoring, particularly within the context of the learning community as this intersects with collaborative reflective inquiry. Among the six types of mentoring support groups discussed in this chapter, arts-based mentoring is by far the least developed. It is anticipated that, over time, arts-based mentoring will be explicitly woven into a wider range of creative activity, such as script-writing and drama, and choreography and dance.

In a pedagogical experiment that used a Monet painting to teach leadership, Barber and colleagues (2001) integrated the arts and mentoring in an educational administration course. The conditions established for a group of prospective school administrators (experienced teachers) centered on the use of an arts-based collective activity called the Monet Project for enacting reflection, engagement, and discovery. Gathering in an art studio instead of his or her usual classroom, each student received a piece of the whole—"1/12th of a reproduction of Monet's *Water Lilies and Japanese Bridge*. . . . Students were not told what the 'big picture' was, although some had an idea that it was a Monet. . . . They went to the center table and selected paints" (p. 29). Each student struggled with the need to perfectly reproduce their own panel, but as the panels were placed side by side, the members sighed in relief upon seeing that the bridge was "clearly evident."

The faculty team used this organic experience of discovery to introduce the concepts of critical thought, positive **synergy**, collaborative mentorship, and collective action. Students felt that they had experienced managerial control differently and, perhaps for the first time, transformational leadership; they had moved from relying on predictive forms of control to engaging in a whole community project through experiential learning. The Monet Project perpetuated endless possibilities for rethinking professional practice and the self from a communal perspective. As a "reformed" discourse community, the class

---

Synergy
producing, through shared efforts, a total effect beyond any individual's particular contribution

members together grappled with new images of leader, including that of risk taker, team player, scholar–practitioner, and lifelong learner.

A Final Word

I hope this chapter has reinforced the message that there exist many synergistic comentoring movements that challenge our technocratic worlds. When technical mentoring complements alternative mentoring, organizations are strengthened and can gradually change.

Finally, it is reassuring to know that some teaching–learning relationships that were once hierarchically defined are now being recast in more egalitarian ways. Studies offer insight into how authoritarian structures can shift when critically reflective, collaboratively oriented communities are at work. The collapse of some traditional mentoring relationship structures has had a pronounced impact in two ways. First, it has forced re-examination of the respective senior–subordinate stance of the mentor, resulting in alternative, more empowering roles, such as taking turns in research duties and sharing rewards. Second, the restructuring and transformation of relationships suggest possibilities that not only improve one-on-one mentoring dyads but also extend well beyond them.

Glossary

Mentoring cohort—faculty–student support group that brings together learners with an academic instructor(s) or dissertation chair(s)

Mentoring leadership—leaders and partners whose creative visions of mentorship help transform organizational relationships and systems

Mentoring (learning) community—formal or informal arrangements that bring together any combination of scholars, practitioners, students, stakeholders, and activists to inquire into practice and promote professional development

Mentoring mosaic—a collegial network of multiple mentors and opportunities for growth

Peer coaching—a collegial learning process whereby educators assist other experienced faculty in a reciprocal exchange

Postmodern—a worldview that confronts metanarratives of truth, stasis, and universal reason and promotes critique, reflection, and empathy

Study group—voluntary membership of students, teachers, or other persons gathering informally or formally to accomplish a short- or long-term goal

Support group—temporary, transitional structures for satisfying human needs and meeting goals, with potential for more established and sustaining forms

Synergy—producing, through shared efforts, a total effect beyond any individual's particular contribution

Telementoring—computer-based mentoring involving online communications where the mentor, a specialist in a field of interest, provides academic or professional guidance to mentees

Questions for Discussion

1. *The Mentorship Primer* presents contradictions between technical and alternative mentoring by introducing the complex, changing world of mentorship. Readers new to the topic may be seeking the greatest possible clarity, and established mentors may be hoping to locate ideas, solutions, and formats for use in their own settings. This text therefore possesses some of the "commodity" features identified with technical mentoring and writing even though its ideological orientation favors educational inquiry and the pursuit of alternatives. Using this insight, (a) identify and analyze the "commodity" features that appear throughout the book; and (b) in chapters 3 and 4, find examples of the author's bias for alternative mentoring as evidenced by word choice and examples.

2. Do you think positive mentoring can become a personal and cultural "habit"—in the Deweyian (1938) sense of forming new "emotional and intellectual" attitudes—within learning organizations? If so, what might be necessary for this to occur within and across systems? Apply your response to a local institutional context that is familiar to you (e.g., a school), and then see how your solutions play out across several different organizational settings. Do your solutions seem to fit only one context, or do they accommodate more general contexts?

3. Participate in a supportive critiquing process with a peer or group on works in progress. Once the activity has been completed, reflect on what was learned technically, cognitively, organizationally, personally, interpersonally, and emotionally. Share your insights with others who can gain from them, such as a class (group) or team (cohort) and disseminate your results.

4. Explore the advantages and disadvantages of both formal and informal cohorts. Talk with members from your own unit or another to learn what best enhances group learning (e.g., diversity in membership, designated peer mentors). Using these insights, write a report about the type of cohort that is needed for a particular group. List the values, factors, or preferences to be considered for designing the cohort. For helpful ideas, consult the literature on cohort partnership and assessment cited in this book (e.g., Horn, 2001).
5. Respond to the following questions, relevant within the scope of lifelong mentoring: What distinguishes lifelong mentorship of an individual from the long-term mentoring activity that occurs within a structured program of an organization? How does the idea of mentoring the elderly practically manifest itself, especially when the mentor is significantly younger than the mentee? By contrast, what innovative forms of mentoring can be proposed by or for adolescents? Do those who have the assurance of having succeeded in their careers (and having even guided others) perceive a need for mentoring?

CHAPTER FIVE

Conclusion

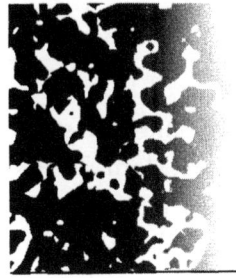

As we know, mentoring does not exist in a vacuum apart from the world, nor is it confined to the pedagogy and authority of one's relationship, classroom, or environment. From this perspective, the following six overarching lessons and implications are apparent from the prolific research on mentoring and related areas of critical, political, and feminist thought.

Lesson 1. Sociocultural, policy, corporate, and economic climates shape the work of teaching and learning in schools as well as universities and businesses. Macro forces actively inform the ideologies and forms of mentoring.

Technical mentoring, an enculturation process that exhibits external control over curriculum as well as teaching and learning dynamics has been engineered for nationwide educational reform. Power blocs have forged political and economic agendas for mentoring based on shared profiteering interests (Steinberg & Kincheloe, 1997a, 1997b), as reflected in such all-encompassing national laws as the *No Child Left Behind Act of 2001* (NCLB)

(U.S. Department of Education, 2002) and high-stakes testing policies (Amrein & Berliner, 2002; Horn, 2004).

Lesson 2. Subtle forces of mythology and metaphor reside within the human psyche and the culture of organizations and play a role in learning and socialization processes as well as professional lives. Myth and metaphor generate unconscious perspectives on and attitudes toward mentoring and broadly inform the actions of mentors and mentees.

In an unusual study, two Israeli groups of beginning high school teachers participated in a mentoring awareness exercise. Action researcher Orland-Barak (2001) found that the novice teachers viewed mentoring as interchangeable with teaching—in other words, mentoring was seen in terms of the more familiar landscape: teaching. This is an example of how metaphors (i.e., mentoring as teaching) can limit one's understanding. Without sufficient knowledge about or experience with mentoring, these teachers appeared to hold a very incomplete and traditional, if not elusive, picture of mentorship.

A related point is that future teachers (and, arguably, school leaders) need assistance in making critical distinctions between teaching and mentoring so they can grow as collaborators, synergistic mentors, and lifelong learners (Herman & Mandell, 2004). This developmental capacity is also important to the collective work of educators and leaders from different types of institutions and walks of life.

Lesson 3. As school and university accountability becomes increasingly regulated at the highest levels of government, degrees of educational freedom are lost. As a consequence of this trend, technical mentoring has been ascribed permanent status in K–12 public schools and colleges as a robust solution for standardizing student learning and teacher performance.

A profound hidden curriculum of national laws mandates that educational systems sponsor the values and interests of corporate America. This has had the effect of shaping an efficiency mindset for faculty and leaders within schools and universities (Horn, 2004; Kincheloe, 1995,

1999, 2004a). Such developments have vigorously reintroduced technical–rational administrative approaches to learning and mentoring that aim to standardize not only student learning but also teacher performance. Such living forms of technocracy as high-stakes testing "frown upon" the self-directed, organic, and political work of teacher communities (Mullen, with Stover & Corley, 2001), replacing these with an "emphasis on individual competition and private property," which "reinforces corporate values" (Ornstein & Levine, 2000, p. 419).

However, some school-based experts view statewide policy groups, including teacher commissions and businesses, as setting a long overdue precedent (albeit without ample guidelines and resources). "New roles and new structures" have been called for "in an attempt to change the social relations of people who do the work at the school level" (Lieberman, Saxl, & Miles, 2000/1988, p. 348). This reform agenda for K–12 schools encourages what is perceived, then, as a movement "from one that fosters privatism and adversarial relationships" between practitioners "to one that encourages collegiality and commitment" (p. 348).

Lesson 4. A more progressive, democratic mentorship ideology and practice is forming in response to technical mentoring. Alternative mentoring appears at the micro level, where the real work—relationships, classrooms, organizations, and communities—is done. Such mentoring is not only an educational concept and practice but also an intentional commitment and political activity.

The evolution of mentoring within schools and other educational institutions is in no way accidental or happenstance. Attracted to the potential profits of mentoring, "superintendents and principals across the nation [over the last 25 years] swept the concept into the systems' and schools' bureaucracy. . . . They established by fiat both immediate and long-range plans for implementation of mentoring" (Davis, 2001, p. 2).

While many mentors and writers recognize that mentorship can be neither mandated nor monitored, this does not imply that mentoring is somehow a **laissez-faire**

Laissez-faire refers here to the philosophy or practice of avoiding planning (not to the doctrine of avoiding government controls in economic affairs) endeavor. It is essential that educators and leaders take responsibility for creating authentic mentoring relationships and for instituting profound change. Solutions for dealing openly with issues of power and authority must include discovery of new ways for us to relate to one another. The challenge here, then, for all who engage in the **mentoring enterprise** is to identify our own personal, political, and ethical orientations and to encourage others to share theirs. Another obstacle involves transcending one's own individual needs to accommodate the larger community (Davis, 2001). Potential pitfalls in the adult mentoring relationship must not only be recognized but also monitored. These include intense dependency of the mentee, male-dominated paradigms and dynamics, power imbalances, unethical behaviors, and intellectual property rights (Tenner, 2004).

> **Mentoring enterprise**
> a venture requiring determination, energy, and initiative on the part of individuals and the collective

The **mentoring ethic** has now been thoroughly absorbed into the national and state policymaking and accountability arenas and specifically into evaluation, accreditation, assessment, credentialing, and other standards-based initiatives that have direct, intentional impact for redesigning the work of educators. Clandinin and Connelly's (1992) empowering metaphor of "teacher as curriculum maker" is being stretched more than ever with this intensification over the last decade of school reform.

> **Mentoring ethic**
> moral standards for human conduct that govern particular acts or activities

Educators who proactively engage in creating alternatives for improving our teaching and learning situations have promising ideas and results to share. Contemporary mentoring projects include networks configured to particular professional needs (Duff, 1999), specialized mentoring programs for faculty of color (Groomes, 1999), experimental co-learning relationships and exercises (Johnson-Bailey & Cervero, 2004), and synergistic comentoring support groups (Lick, 1999a).

Finally, while technical and alternative mentoring may appear to be bipolar in theory, in practice they can overlap. The artificial lines that separate them will often blur, rendering technical and alternative mentoring indistinguishable at times. Nonetheless, fine distinctions between technical and alternative mentoring can be made through communal discourse, reflective analysis, and explorations of context.

Lesson 5. Mentoring, although becoming recognized for its value as a change force at even the executive levels of organizations and governments, is nonetheless insufficiently rewarded. At the same time, the proactive expectation for mentoring activity requires personal time and energy to assist learners or colleagues and hence depends on mentors "going above and beyond." Needed, then, are wholesale reward structures.

Many higher education institutions have failed to "assign" mentoring as a faculty duty with recognition and reward structures (Clark, Harden, & Johnson, 2000). It is not only within universities that faculty are expected to rise to the occasion of mentoring without sufficient support. America's public schools have also struggled to sustain teachers as instructional mentors when state funding is abruptly cut off or shortchanged (Mullen & Slagle, 2004).

In the telementoring context, some of the lack of acceptance toward electronic course delivery in higher education comes from faculty who are not technology experts. Significant training beyond one's areas of academic specialization is required in technology and pedagogy. As Karlen (2001) argues, such new modes of course delivery demand a rethinking of instructional preparation time, teaching load, class size, contact hours, feedback, and incentives and rewards. Further compounding this problem, senior faculty are generally less technologically invested and knowledgeable in this respect. Consequently, the responsibility for electronic course design and delivery is placed on the shoulders of tenure-earning and adjunct faculty as well as those willing to retool (Mullen, 2005).

Doctoral supervision, an even more complex and demanding mentoring activity, involves a long-term commitment to individual university students. Professors who are dissertation supervisors, then, bear a great deal of mentoring responsibility and are thus more harshly impacted by lack of incentive or compensation. This situation also extends to master's thesis students and those involved in time-intensive independent studies and special projects, including faculty support of publication of student-authored works.

Lesson 6. Mentoring, a holistic form of teaching and learning, embraces the professional and the personal, the psychosocial and career facets of a protégé's development, and such activities as advising, tutoring, coaching, and counseling. Also, mentoring has special qualities, notably the developmental opportunity involving mentors and mentees in learning partnerships as well as structured and informal activity settings, traditional dyads recast as comentoring relationships and support group structures, and the epistemology of learning itself as a lifelong commitment.

There are many ways in which the concept and act of mentoring have perhaps been misunderstood. To clarify, someone may be a fine lecturer or teacher but not necessarily a good mentor. And some qualified, experienced faculty forego mentoring students outside the formal classroom context due to the lack of institutional support previously described. It is also important to note that many faculty lack a fundamental interest in mentoring—some bereft of the vision, drive, or energy while others are inclined to perform as minimally as possible.

Further, a major source of misunderstanding involves how mentorship itself has been conceptualized in the educational field. Simply put, mentoring concepts and practices continue to be grouped with those of induction and supervision. Teacher induction is restricted to the transitional processes and systems required for new teachers (Gottesman, 2000), and teacher supervision focuses on "supervisors as developers and leaders of leaders" (Sergiovanni & Starratt, 1998, p. 4). In this context, the mentoring phenomenon arguably embraces both induction and supervision.

Mentoring is also associated with a broader, deeper, and more lasting commitment, at least on the part of the **authentic mentor**. In addition, mentors who impose tight parameters and thereby fall short of helping their mentees—or those who act unethically, thus compromising the integrity of the relationship and the mentee's own

Authentic mentor
an identification bestowed upon an individual by another

well-being—are *not* considered true mentors, even in the definitional sense. According to studies that have been conducted, more than 10% of graduate students who are mentees have ethical concerns about their mentor relationships, something that all students should be mindful of as they search for faculty members who demonstrate honesty, fairness, and integrity (Clark, et al., 2000). Also, all mentees and supervisory leaders of faculty mentors will need to monitor the all-too-familiar situation involving ineffective mentors who are ethical but fail to fulfill the human contract and accomplish the necessary goals. Further, because authentic mentors model self-awareness and have healthy boundaries, they are able to address dysfunctionality in their protégés' work habits, which can range from poor writing standards, to erratic spurts of productivity, to self-imposed social isolation. At the same time, they have empathy for their protégés and the constant challenge of what is for them new learning. Importantly, "good mentors" know how to balance honesty with empowerment; they talk openly with their students in order to promote positive change while avoiding using power over them, which has the effect of diminishing their self-esteem (Johnson & Huwe, 2003).

It is worth remembering that some capable professionals as well as feminist scholars (e.g., Darwin, 2000) dislike the word *mentor*. Some say the word has a paternal connotation, which is an accurate observation, considering its etymology and history within the professions as "man's work." *Mentor* means "adviser" in Greek and comes from the Indo-European root *men*, meaning "to think" or "mind" (*The American Heritage Dictionary of the English Language*, Third Edition, 1992, Houghton Mifflin; also, see "Mentor," http://www.psu.edu/dus/mentor/homer, 2004). Given the logical inference that "mentor" has been endorsed as the exclusive terrain of intelligent males, many understandably shy away from this term.

However, our collective actions as educators, particularly within recent years, have reclaimed the act of mentoring, imbuing it with credibility. Most seasoned female professionals have not only experienced the role of mentoring in one way or another but also have initiated a new wave of intergenerational woman-to-woman and race-based mentoring networks (Duff, 1999; Kasprisin, Single, Single, & Muller, 2003; Packard, Walsh, & Seidenberg, 2004). As a parallel development, more and more veteran male professionals currently engage in cross-cultural (gender and race) mentoring and even welcome the opportunity to do so (Clark et al., 2000; Dreher & Chargois, 1998). Such actions perpetuate new mentoring legacies or successions of ideas, practices, and values (Tenner, 2004). Mentors, leaders, and partners alike have effected systemic change beyond relationship rescripting in such forms as policy, leadership, collaboration, and instructional mentorship. As a change force, then, mentorship is contributing to the contemporary dream of a full and complete equality for all teachers and learners.

In its support of a psychosocial approach to learning and education, alternative mentoring also contributes an "epistemology of affect" (e.g., Herman & Mandell, 2004, p. 137). Theorizing about emotion, researchers have reflected on the role of **cognitive love** in creating strong, ethical relationships. They also see that affect has value specifically in forming and appreciating attachments, risking encounters, exposing vulnerabilities, creating interdependence, prolonging learning, and developing independence (Herman & Mandell, 2004; Hoyle, 2002). Some consider mentoring to be an experience in professional friendship—others in transformative learning, still others in paradigm revitalization. But a broader view of mentorship is as a cycle that repeats in people's work and lives.

All in all, the word *mentor* offers a powerful example of how our collective literary roots live on without our even knowing it—often in new, hopeful, and splendid forms.

Cognitive love
the desire to learn as driven by the need for love, attachment, and understanding

Glossary

Authentic mentor—an identification bestowed upon an individual by another

Cognitive love—the desire to learn as driven by the need for love, attachment, and understanding

Laissez-faire—refers here to the philosophy or practice of avoiding planning (not to the doctrine of avoiding government controls in economic affairs)

Mentoring enterprise—a venture requiring determination, energy, and initiative on the part of individuals and the collective

Mentoring ethic—moral standards for human conduct that govern particular acts or activities

Questions for Discussion

1. Refresh your memory of the *Mentorship Primer* by flipping through chapters 1 through 4 to build on the six lessons briefly described in this chapter about teaching and learning (and education more generally). Other lessons have also been made available in this book that you can narrate in an abbreviated form.
2. List your "significant learnings" from this book. What did you learn that you might not have previously known? With whom can you share your insight and with what imagined effect or outcome? Try this exercise and compare what you had hoped might transpire from the exchange with what actually occurred.
3. Read French theologian and writer Fénelon's (François de Salignac de la Mothe) romance *Les Aventures de Télémaque* (1699), available in English as *The Adventures of Telemachus*. This novel, condemned by Pope Innocent XII, portrays the journey of the son of Ulysses with Mentor (*Columbia Encyclopedia*, http://www.bartleby.com/65/fe/Fenelon, 2004). Speculate as to why it was condemned. Would you condemn it today? Why?

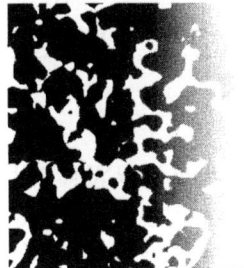

References and Resources

In my approach to the *Mentorship Primer*, I completed a comprehensive review in 2004 of the education and business literature, ranging from historic works (1970s) to current texts. The primary themes that emerged were *foundations of mentoring* (philosophical, historical, and epistemological) and *frameworks of mentoring* (technical mentoring and alternative mentoring). The data (key words and phrases) from the literature were color coded and displayed in charts to organize the writing of this book.

Over 600 articles, commentaries, books, and monographs, including nonprint (electronic) sources, were analyzed. I summarized and synthesized qualitative as well as quantitative studies, utilizing mixed research methods. For the themes that were identified, the following areas were covered: the authors' conceptualization (e.g., perspective, framework, politics, and language), context (school, university, or corporate), and application of mentoring (e.g., relational, program, and network).

Print Resources

Adams, N. (1996). *Piano lessons: Music, love & true adventure.* New York: Dell.

Allen, T. D., & Finkelstein, L. M. (2003). Beyond mentoring: Alternative sources and functions of developmental support. *Career Development Quarterly, 51*(4), 346–355.

Almog, T., & Hertz-Lazarowitz, R. (1999). Teachers as peer learners: Professional development in an advanced computer learning environment. In A. M. O'Donnell & A. King (Eds.), *Cognitive perspectives on peer learning* (pp. 285–311). Mahwah, NJ: Lawrence Erlbaum.

Amrein, A., & Berliner, D. C. (2002). High-stakes testing, uncertainty, and student learning. *Education Policy Analysis Archives, 10*(18), 1–20. [Online]. Retrieved on July 3, 2004 from http://epaa.asu.edu/epaa/v10n18.

Anderson, E. M., & Shannon, A. L. (1988). Toward a conceptualization of mentoring. *Journal of Teacher Education, 39*(1), 38–42.

Arizona Education Association. (2003, February). *Arizona Academic Standards.* [Online]. Retrieved on August 17, 2004 from http://www.arizonaea.org/PDFs/ aimsbklt.pdf

Avis, J., Bathmaker, A–M., Kendal, A., & Parsons, J. (2003). Conundrums of our own making: Critical pedagogy and trainee further education teachers. *Teacher Development, 7*(2), 191–209.

Banks, C. (2000). Gender and race as factors in educational leadership and administration In Jossey-Bass Publishers (Ed.), *The Jossey-Bass reader on educational leadership* (pp. 217–256). San Francisco, CA: Jossey-Bass.

Barber, E., Chandler, S., & Collins, E. C. (2001). Using Monet to teach leadership: Integrating the arts into educational administration preparation. *Journal of Curriculum Theorizing, 17*(2), 27–38.

Beyene, T., Anglin, M., Sanchez, W., & Ballou, M. (2002). Mentoring and relational mutuality: Protégés' perspectives. *Journal of Humanistic Counseling, Education and Development, 41*(1), 87–102.

Bingham, S. C., Finney, P. B., & Hood, A. (2000). Designing school leadership development programmes: Recommendations from the SERVE Leaders Institute, *The AASA Professor, 23*(3), 13–19. [Online]. Available: http://www.aasa.org.

Blake-Beard, S. D. (2001). Taking a hard look at formal mentoring programs: A consideration of potential challenges facing women. *Journal of Management Development, 20*(4), 331–345.

Blasé, J., & Blasé, J. (2000). Effective instructional leadership: Teachers' perspectives on how principals promote teaching and learning in schools. *Journal of Educational Administration, 38*(2), 130–141.

Bloom, G., & Krovetz, M. (2001). A step into the principalship. *Leadership, 30*(3), 12–13.

Bobbitt, F. (1918). *The curriculum*. Cambridge, MA: The Riverside Press.

Bona, M. J., Rinehart, J., & Volbrecht, R. M. (1995). "Show me how to do like you: Comentoring as feminist pedagogy. *Feminist Teacher*, 9(3), 116–124.

Borja, R. R. (2001). Growing their own. *Richmond Times Dispatch*, 1–4. [Online]. Retrieved on June 23, 2004 from http://www.timesdispatch.com.

Bruffee, K. A. (1999). *Collaborative learning: Higher education, interdependence, and the authority of knowledge* (2nd ed.). Baltimore, MD: Johns Hopkins University Press.

Bruner, D. Y., & Livingston, M. (2002). Out of the mouth of babes. *Journal of Cases in Educational Leadership*, 5(1), 1–11. [Online]. Retrieved on July 18, 2004 from http://www.ucea.org/cases.

Brunner, C. C. (2002). Professing educational leadership: Conceptions of power. *Journal of School Leadership*, 12(6) 693–720.

Caputo-Pearl, A. (2001). Challenging high-stakes standardized testing: Working to build an anti-racist, progressive social movement in public education. *Taboo: Journal of Culture and Education*, 5(1), 87–121.

Carnegie, D. (1936/1998). *How to win friends & influence people*. New York: Pocket Books.

Carnegie Forum on Education and the Economy, Task Force on Teaching as a Profession. (1986). *A nation prepared: Teachers for the 21st century*. New York: Carnegie Corporation. (ERIC Document Reproduction Service NO. ED 268120)

Carver, C. L. (2003). The principal's role in new teacher induction. In M. Scherer (Ed.), *Keeping good teachers* (pp. 1–12). Alexandria, VA: Association for Supervision and Curriculum Development. [Online]. Retrieved on June 20, 2004 from http://www.ascd.org/publications/books/2003scherer/carverch4.

Chao, G. T., Waltz, P. M., & Gardner, P. D. (1992). Formal and informal mentorships: A comparison of mentoring functions and contrast with nonmentored counterparts. *Personnel Psychology*, 45, 619–316.

Christiansen, H., & Ramadevi, S. (Eds.). (2002). *Reeducating the educator: Global perspectives on community building*. Albany, NY: State University of New York Press.

Clandinin, D. J., & Connelly, F. M. (1992). Teacher as curriculum maker. In P. W. Jackson (Ed.), *Handbook of research on curriculum* (pp. 340–363). New York: Macmillan.

Clandinin, D. J., & Connelly, F. M. (1995). *Teachers' professional knowledge landscapes*. New York: Teachers College Press.

Clark, R. A., Harden, S. L., & Johnson, W. B. (2000). Mentor relationships in clinical psychology doctoral training: Results of a national survey. *Teaching of Psychology*, 27(4), 262–268.

Clopton, R. W., & Ou, T-C. (1973). *John Dewey: Lectures in China, 1919–1920*. Honolulu: University Press of Hawaii.

Clutterbuck, D., & Ragins, B. R. (2001). *Mentoring and diversity: An international perspective.* Burlington, MA: Butterworth–Heinemann.

Connelly, F. M., & Clandinin, D. J. (1988). *Teachers as curriculum planners: Narratives of experience.* New York: Teachers College Press.

Conner, D. R. (1993). *Managing at the speed of change.* New York: Villard.

Covey, S. R. (1989). *The seven habits of highly effective people.* New York: Simon & Schuster.

Crow, G. M., & Glascock, C. (1995). Socialization to a new conception of the principalship. *Journal of Educational Administration, 33*(1), 22–43.

Danielson, C., & McGreal, T. L. (2000). *Teacher evaluation to enhance professional practice.* Alexandria, VA: Association for Supervision and Curriculum Development.

Darling-Hammond, L., & Sykes, G. (2003). Wanted: A national teacher supply policy for education: The right way to meet the "highly qualified teacher" challenge. *Education Policy Analysis Archives, 11*(33), 1–55. [Online]. Retrieved on June 30, 2004 from http://epaa.asu.edu/epaa/v11n33.

Darwin, A. (2000). Critical reflections on mentoring in work settings. *Adult Education Quarterly, 50*(3), 197–211.

Davis, O. L., Jr. (2001). Editorial: A view of authentic mentorship. *Journal of Curriculum and Supervision, 17*(1), 1–4.

Dembowski, F. L. (1988). What should we do now? Suggested directions for school administration programs. *The AASA Professor, 22*(1), 1–7. [Online]. Retrieved on July 17, 2004 from http://www.aasa.org.

Dewey, J. (1916/1997). *Democracy and education: An introduction to the philosophy of education.* New York: Macmillan.

Dewey, J. (1938). *Experience and education.* New York: Macmillan.

Diamond, C. T. P., & Mullen, C. A. (Eds.). (1999a). *The postmodern educator: Arts-based inquiries and teacher development.* New York: Peter Lang.

Diamond, C. T. P., & Mullen, C. A. (1999b). "Roped together": Artistic forms of comentoring in higher education (pp. 315–340). In C. T. P. Diamond & C. A. Mullen (Eds.), *The postmodern educator: Arts-based inquiries and teacher development.* New York: Peter Lang.

Dinham, S., & Scott, C. (2001). The experience of disseminating the results of doctoral research. *Journal of Further and Higher Education, 25*(1), 45–55.

Dorn, S., & Papalewis, R. (1997). *Improving doctoral student retention.* Paper presented at the Annual Meeting of the American Educational Research Association, Chicago.

Dreher, G. F., & Chargois, J. A. (1998). Gender, mentoring experiences, and salary attainment among graduates of an historically black university. *Journal of Vocational Behavior, 53,* 401–416.

Duff, C. S. (1999). *Learning from other women.* New York: AMACOM American Management Association.

DuFour, R., & Eaker, R. (1998). *Professional learning communities at work: Best practices for enhancing student achievement*. Alexandria, VA: Association for Supervision and Curriculum Development.

Eby, L. T. (1997). Alternative forms of mentoring in changing organizational environments: A conceptual extension of the mentoring literature. *Journal of Vocational Behavior, 51*(1), 125–144.

Effective leaders for today's schools: Synthesis of a policy forum on educational leadership. (1999, June). Policy brief retrieved from http://www.ed.gov/pubs/EffectiveLeaders/policy-forum.html on October 15, 2002.

Eisner, E. W. (1996). Is 'the art of teaching' a metaphor? In M. Kompf, W. R. Bond, D. Dworet, & R. T. Boak (Eds.), *Changing research and practice: Teachers' professionalism, identities, and knowledge* (pp. 9–19). London: Falmer.

English, F. W. (2003a). Cookie-cutter leaders for cookie-cutter schools: The teleology of standardization and the de-legitimization of the university in educational leadership preparation. *Leadership and Policy in Schools*, 1–20.

English, F. W. (2003b). *The postmodern challenge to the theory and practice of educational administration*. Springfield, IL: Charles C. Thomas.

Flinders, D. J., & Thornton, S. J. (2004). Preface to the second edition. In D. J. Flinders & S. J. Thornton (Eds.), *The curriculum studies reader* (2nd ed.) (pp. viiii-x). New York: Routledge.

Flinders, D. J., & Thornton, S. J. (Eds.). (2004). *The curriculum studies reader* (2nd ed.). New York: Routledge.

Flockhart, K., & Woloshyn, V. E. (2001). Enhancing first-time teaching at the postsecondary level: A story of collaborative mentorship (pp. 39–51). In H. E. Christiansen & S. Ramadevi (Eds.), *Reeducating the educator: Global perspectives on community building*. Albany, NY: State University of New York Press.

Florida Department of Education. (2003, June 17). *The BEST proposal*. (Jim Horne, Commissioner.) [Online]. Retrieved on March 13, 2004 from http://www.fldoe. org/meetings/June_17_03/BEST_Proposal_Item.

Florida Senate, The. (2003). *The 2003 Florida Statutes*. Title XLVIII, K–20 Education Code: Assessment Procedures and Criteria, F.S. 1012.34(a) and 1012.231. [Online]. Retrieved on April 24, 2004 from http://www.flsenate.gov/Statutes/index.

Freire, P. (1997). A response. In P. Freire, with J. W. Fraser, D. Macedo, T. McKinnon, & W. T. Stokes (Eds.), *Mentoring the mentor: A critical dialogue with Paulo Freire* (pp. 303–329). New York: Peter Lang.

Fullan, M. (1999). *Change forces: The sequel*. London: Sage.

Furlong, J., & Maynard, T. (1995). *Mentoring student teachers*. London, England: Routledge.

Furman, G. C. (1998). Postmodernism and community in schools: Unravelling the paradox. *Educational Administration Quarterly, 34*(3), 298–328.

Furtwengler, C. B. (1995). Beginning teachers programs: Analysis of state actions during the reform era. *Education Policy Analysis Archives*, 3(3), 1–20. [Online]. Retrieved on June 30, 2004 from http://epaa.asu.edu/epaa/v3n3.

Futrell, M. (2003). Teaching tomorrow's citizens today: The need for more highly qualified teachers. *Teacher Education & Practice*, 16(4), 355–369.

Gallimore, R. G., Tharp, R. G., & John-Steiner, V. (1992). *The developmental and sociocultural foundations of mentoring*. Columbia University, New York: Institute for Urban Minority Education. (ERIC Document Reproduction Service No. ED 354292)

Geber, H. (2003). Fostering career development for black academics in the new South Africa. In F. K. Kochan & J. T. Pascarelli (Eds.), *Global perspectives on mentoring: Transforming contexts, communities, and cultures* (pp. 107–128). (Series: *Perspectives in mentoring, II*). Greenwich, CT: Information Age.

Giroux, H. A. (1996). *Living dangerously: Multiculturalism and the politics of differences*. New York: Peter Lang.

Glanz, J. (1990). Beyond bureaucracy: Notes on the professionalization of public school supervision in the early 20th century. *Journal of Curriculum and Supervision*, 5(2), 150–170.

Glickman, C. (1998). Educational leadership for democratic purpose: What do we mean? *International Journal of Leadership in Education*, 1(1), 47–53.

Goldring, E. B. (1992). System-wide diversity in Israel: Principals as transformational and environmental leaders. *Journal of Educational Administration*, 39(3), 49–62.

Gottesman, B. (2000). *Peer coaching for educators* (2nd ed.). Lanham, MA: Scarecrow.

Grogan, M. (2004). Keeping a critical, postmodern eye on educational leadership in the United States: In appreciation of Bill Foster. *Educational Administration Quarterly*, 40(2), 222–239.

Groomes, F. L. (1999). The league of mentors: A strategy beyond the faculty handbook. In C. A. Mullen & D. W. Lick (Eds.), *New directions in mentoring: Creating a culture of synergy* (pp. 79–86). London, England: Falmer.

Gross, R. A. (2002, February 28). From 'old boys' to mentors. *Chronicle of Higher Education*, 1–5. [Online]. Retrieved on June 28, 2004 from http://chronicle.com/jobs/2002/02/2002022801c.

Hamilton, E. (1940/1969). *Mythology: Timeless tales of gods and heroes*. New York: Little, Brown & Company.

Hargreaves, A., & Fullan, M. (2000). Mentoring in the new millennium. *Theory into Practice*, 39(1), 50–56.

Head, F. A., Reiman, A. J., & Thies-Sprinthall, L. (1992). The reality of mentoring: Complexity in its process and function. In T. M. Bey, & C. T. Holmes (Eds.), *Mentoring: Contemporary principles and issues* (pp. 5–34). Reston, VA: Association of Teacher Educators.

Henrich, K. T. (1991). Loving partnerships: Dealing with sexual attraction and power in doctoral advisement relationships. *Journal of Higher Education, 62*(5), 514–538.

Herman, L., & Mandell, A. (2004). *From teaching to mentoring: Principle and practice, dialogue and life in adult education.* London: RoutledgeFalmer.

Homer. (1998/2000). *The Odyssey.* (R. Fitzgerald, trans., sixth printing). New York: Farrar, Straus, & Giroux.

Hopkins, D., & Levin, B. (2000). Government policy and school development. *School Leadership & Management, 20*(1), 15–30.

Horn, Jr., R. A. (2001). Promoting social justice and caring in schools and communities: The unrealized potential of the cohort model. *Journal of School Leadership, 11,* 313–334.

Horn, Jr., R. A. (2002). Differing perspectives on the magic of dialogue: Implications for a scholar-practitioner leader. *Scholar-Practitioner Quarterly, 1*(2), 83–102.

Horn, Jr., R. A. (2004). *The standards primer.* New York: Peter Lang.

Howe, K. (1997). *Understanding equal educational opportunity: Social justice, democracy, and schooling.* New York: Teachers College Press.

Hoyle, J. (2002). *Leadership and the force of love: Six keys to motivating with love.* Thousand Oaks, CA: Corwin.

Jaffee, D. (2004, July 9). Learning communities can be cohesive—and divisive. *Chronicle of Higher Education, 50*(44), B16.

Janesick, V. J. (2003). *Curriculum trends: A reference handbook.* Denver, CO: ABC–CLIO.

Jipson, J., & Paley, N. (2000). Because no one gets there alone: Collaboration as co-mentoring. *Theory Into Practice, 39*(1), 36–42.

Johnson, W. B., & Huwe, J. M. (2003). *Getting mentored in graduate school.* Washington, DC: American Psychological Association.

Johnson-Bailey, J., & Cervero, R. M. (2004). Mentoring in black and white: The intricacies of cross-cultural mentoring. *Mentoring & Tutoring, 12*(1), 7–21.

Jones, B. A. (1992). Collaboration: The case for indigenous community-based organization support of dropout prevention programming and implementation. *Journal of Negro Education, 61*(4), 496–508.

Kardos, S. M., Johnson, S. M., Deske, H. G., Kauffman, D., & Liu, E. (2001). Counting on colleagues: New teachers encounter the professional cultures of their schools. *Educational Administration Quarterly, 37*(2), 250–290.

Kariuki, M., Franklin, T., & Duran, M. (2001). A technology partnership: Lessons learned by mentors. *Journal of Technology and Teacher Education, 9*(3), 407–417.

Karlen, J. M. (2001). Accreditation and assessment in distance learning. *Academic Leadership, 1*(4), 1–6. [Online]. Retrieved on July 28, 2004 from http://www.academicleadership.org.

Kasprisin, C. A., Single, P. B., Single, R. M., & Muller, C. B. (2003). Building a better bridge: Testing e-training to improve e-mentoring programs for diversity in higher education. *Mentoring & Tutoring, 11*(1), 67–78.

Kea, C. D., Penny, J. M., & Bowman, L. J. (2003). The experiences of African American students in special education master's programs at traditionally white institutions. *Teacher Education and Special Education, 26*(4), 273–287.

Kealy, W. A., & Mullen, C. A. (2003a). Guest editors' introduction: At the nexus of mentoring and technology. [Special issue]. *Mentoring & Tutoring, 11*(1), 3–13.

Kealy, W. A., & Mullen, C. A. (2003b). Guest editor of "Mentoring & technology: Exploring the nexus." [Special issue]. *Mentoring & Tutoring, 11*(1), 1–121.

Kelehear, Z. (2003). Mentoring the organization: Helping principals bring schools to higher levels of effectiveness. *NASSP Bulletin, 87*, 35–47.

Kincheloe, J. L. (1995). *Toil and trouble: Good work, smart workers, and the integration of academic and vocational education.* New York: Peter Lang.

Kincheloe, J. L. (1999). *How do we tell the workers?: The socioeconomic foundations of work and vocational education.* Boulder, CO: Westview.

Kincheloe, J. L. (2004a). *The critical pedagogy primer.* New York: Peter Lang.

Kincheloe, J. L. (2004b). The knowledges of teacher education: Developing a critical complex epistemology. *Teacher Education Quarterly, 31*(1), 49–66.

Kincheloe, J. L., & Steinberg, S. R. (1995). Introduction: The more questions we ask, the more questions we ask. In J. L. Kincheloe & S. R. Steinberg (Eds.), *Thirteen questions: Reframing education's conversation* (2nd ed., pp. 1–11). New York: Peter Lang.

Kochan, F. K. (Ed.). (2002). *The organizational and human dimensions of successful mentoring programs and relationships.* (Series: Perspectives in mentoring, I). Greenwich, CT: Information Age.

Kochan, F. K., & Pascarelli, J. T. (Eds.). (2003). *Global perspectives on mentoring: Transforming contexts, communities, and cultures.* (Series: Perspectives in mentoring, II). Greenwich, CT: Information Age.

Kram, K. E. (1985/1988). *Mentoring at work: Developmental relationships in organizational life.* Lanham, MA: University Press of America. (Originally published by Scott, Foresman and Company in Glenview, IL.)

Lakoff, G., & Johnson, M. (1980). *Metaphors we live by.* Chicago: University of Chicago Press.

Levinson, D. (1979). *The seasons of a man's life.* New York: Ballantine Books.

Lick, D. W. (1999a). Proactive comentoring relationships: Enhancing effectiveness through synergy. In C. A. Mullen & D. W. Lick (Eds.), *New directions in mentoring: Creating a culture of synergy* (pp. 34–45). London, England: Falmer.

Lick, D. W. (1999b). Multiple level comentoring: Moving toward a learning organization. In C. A. Mullen & D. W. Lick (Eds.), *New directions in mentoring: Creating a culture of synergy* (pp. 202–212). London, England: Falmer.

Lieberman, A., Saxl, E. R., & Miles, M. B. (2000/1988). Teacher leadership: Ideology and practice. In Jossey-Bass (Ed.), *The Jossey-Bass reader on educational leadership* (pp. 348–365). San Francisco, CA: Jossey-Bass.

Lind, S. A. (2003). *Teachers' perceptions of culture in low and high attrition schools.* Unpublished doctoral dissertation, University of South Florida, Tampa.

Lortie, D. C. (1998, Summer). Teaching educational administration: Reflections on our craft. *Journal of Cases in Educational Leadership, 1*(1), 1–12. [Online]. Retrieved on July 1, 2004 from http://www.ucea.org/cases.

Malone, J. (2001). Principal mentoring. *Research Roundup, 17*(2), 1–8. [Online]. (ERIC Clearinghouse on Educational Management, OR). [Online]. Retrieved on June 23, 2004 from http://eric.uoregon.edu/publications/roundup/Winter_2001.

Marsh, D. D. (2000). In Jossey-Bass Publishers (Ed.), Educational leadership for the twenty-first century. *The Jossey-Bass reader on educational leadership* (pp. 126–145). San Francisco, CA: Jossey-Bass.

Maslow, A. (1962). *Toward a psychology of being.* New York: Van Nostrand.

Maynard, T. (2000). Learning to teach or learning to manage mentors? Experience of school-based teacher training. *Mentoring & Tutoring, 8*(1), 17–30.

McCarthy, M. M. (1999). How are school leaders prepared? *Educational Horizons, 77*(2), 74–81.

McDaniel, E. L. (1999). The principal as mentor: From divergence to convergence. In C. A. Mullen & D. W. Lick (Eds.), *New directions in mentoring: Creating a culture of synergy* (pp. 116–124). London, England: Falmer.

McIntyre, A. (1997). *Making meaning of whiteness: Exploring racial identity with white teachers.* Albany, NY: State University of New York Press.

McLaren, P. (1994). *Life in schools: An introduction to critical pedagogy in the foundations of education* (2nd ed.). New York: Longman.

McLaren, P. (2001). *Che Guevara, Paulo Freire, and the pedagogy of revolution.* Boulder, CO: Rowman & Littlefield.

Merriam, S. B. (1983). Mentors and protégés: A critical review of the literature. *Adult Education Quarterly, 33,* 161–173.

Meyer, T. (2002, Fall). Novice teacher learning communities: An alternative to one-on-one mentoring. *American Secondary Education, 31*(1), pp. 27–42.

Mirza, N. (2003). A case for leadership, relationships, and school change in Pakistan. In F. K. Kochan & J. T. Pascarelli (Eds.), *Global perspectives on mentoring: Transforming contexts, communities, and cultures* (pp. 253–271). (Series: *Perspectives in mentoring, II*). Greenwich, CT: Information Age.

Moon, B., & Mayes, A. S. (1995). Integrating values into the assessment of teachers in initial education and training. In T. Kerry & A. S. Mayes (Eds.), *Issues in mentoring* (pp. 233–242). London: Routledge.

Mullen, C. A. (2000). Constructing co-mentoring partnerships: Walkways we must travel. *Theory into Practice, 39*(1), 4–11.

Mullen, C. A. (2004). *Climbing the Himalayas of school leadership: The socialization of early career administrators.* Lanham, MA: Scarecrow.

Mullen, C. A. (2005). *Fire and ice: Igniting and channeling passion in new qualitative researchers.* New York: Peter Lang.

Mullen, C. A., Gordon, S. P., Greenlee, B., & Anderson, R. H. (2002). Capacities for school leadership: Emerging trends in the literature. *International Journal of Educational Reform, 11*(2), 158–198.

Mullen, C. A., & Graves, T. H. (2000). A case study of democratic accountability and school improvement. *Journal of School Leadership, 10*(6), 478–504.

Mullen, C. A., & Kealy, W. A. (1999). Lifelong mentoring: The creation of learning relationships. In C. A. Mullen & D. W. Lick (Eds.), *New directions in mentoring: Creating a culture of synergy* (pp. 187–199). London, England: Falmer.

Mullen, C. A., with Kohan, A. R. (2002). Beyond dualism, splits, and schisms: Social justice for a renewal of vocational–academic education. *Journal of School Leadership, 12*(6), 640–662.

Mullen, C. A., & Lick, D. W. (Eds.). (1999). *New directions in mentoring: Creating a culture of synergy.* London, England: Falmer.

Mullen, C. A., & Slagle, K. R. (2004). *Teacher perceptions of systems-driven quality teaching initiatives: A case exemplar from Florida.* Unpublished paper.

Mullen, C. A., with Stover L., & Corley, B. (2001). School accreditation and teacher empowerment: An Alabama case. *Teacher Development, 5*(1), 101–117.

Mullen, C. A., with Sullivan, E. C. (2002). The New Millennium High School, tomorrow's school today? *International Journal of Leadership in Education, 5*(3), 273–284.

Murphy, J., & Forsyth, P. B. (1999). A decade of change: An overview. In J. Murphy & P. B. Forsyth (Eds.), *Educational administration: A decade of reform* (pp. 3–38). Thousand Oaks, CA: Corwin.

National Commission on Excellence in Education. (1983). *A nation at risk: The imperative for educational reform.* Washington, DC: United States Department of Education.

Noddings, N. (1995). *Philosophy of education.* Boulder, CO: Westview.

Nyquist, J. D., Manning, L., Wulff, D. H., Austin, A. E., Sprague, J., Fraser, P. K., Calcagno, C., & Woodford, B. (1999). On the road to becoming a professor: The graduate student experience. *Change, 31*(3), 18–27.

Nyquist, J. D., & Woodford, B. J. (2000). *Re-envisioning the Ph.D.: What concerns do we have?* Seattle, WA: Center for Instructional Development and Research and the University of Washington.

Oakes, J., Selvin, M., Karoly, L., & Guiton, G. (1992). *Educational matchmaking: Academic and vocational tracking in comprehensive high schools.* Berkeley, CA: National Center for Research in Vocational Education.

Oliver, R. (2003). Assistant principal job satisfaction and desire to become principals. *NCPEA Education Leadership Review, 4*(2), 38–46.

Orland-Barak, L. (2001). Learning to mentor as learning a second language of teaching. *Cambridge Journal of Education, 31*(1), 53–68.

Ornstein, A. C., & Levine, D. U. (2000). *Foundations of education* (7th ed.). New York: Houghton Mifflin.

Orpen, C. (1997). The effects of formal mentoring on employee work motivation, organizational commitment and job performance. *The Learning Organization, 4*(2), 53–60.

Packard, B. W-L., Walsh, L., & Seidenberg, S. (2004). Will that be one mentor or two? A cross-sectional study of women's mentoring during college. *Mentoring & Tutoring, 12*(1), 71–85.

Parkay, F. W., & Stanford, B. H. (2004). *Becoming a teacher* (6th ed.). Boston: Allyn and Bacon.

Paulus, P. B., & Nijstad, B. A. (2003). *Group creativity: Innovation through collaboration.* New York: Oxford University Press.

Payne, R. K. (1998). *A framework for understanding poverty.* Highlands, TX: RFT Publishing.

Piantanida, M., & Garman, N. B. (1999). *The qualitative dissertation: A guide for students and faculty.* Thousand Oaks, CA: Corwin.

Pinar, W. F. (1995/1996). Preface and acknowledgements. In W. F. Pinar, W. M. Reynolds, P. Slattery, & P. M. Taubman (Eds.), *Understanding curriculum: An introduction to the study of historical and contemporary curriculum discourses* (pp. xiii-xviii), New York: Peter Lang.

Pinar, W. F., Reynolds, W. M., Slattery, P., & Taubman, P. M. (1995/1996). *Understanding curriculum: An introduction to the study of historical and contemporary curriculum discourses.* New York: Peter Lang.

Portner, H. (1998). *Mentoring new teachers.* Thousand Oaks, CA: Corwin.

Portner, H. (2001). *Training mentors is not enough.* Thousand Oaks, CA: Corwin.

Portner, H. (2002). *Being mentored: A guide for protégés.* Thousand Oaks, CA: Sage.

Posner, G. (1992). *Analyzing the curriculum.* New York: McGraw-Hill.

Riehl, C. J. (2000). The principal's role in creating inclusive schools for diverse students: A review of normative, empirical, and critical literature on the practice of educational administration. *Review of Educational Research, 70*(1), 55–81.

Rix, M., & Gold, J. (2000). 'With a little help from my academic friend': Mentoring change agents. *Mentoring & Tutoring*, 8(1), 47–62.

Roberts, M. P. (2001). *Your mentor: A practical guide for first-year teachers in grades 1–3*. Thousand Oaks, CA: Corwin.

Rymer, J. (2002). "Only connect": Transforming ourselves and our discipline through co-mentoring. *Journal of Business Communication*, 39(3), 342–363.

Sarason, S. B. (1993). *The case for change: Rethinking the preparation of educators*. San Francisco, CA: Jossey-Bass.

Schmidt, L. (2002). *Gardening in the minefield: A survival guide for school administrators*. Portsmouth, NH: Heinemann.

Schön, D. (1987). *Educating the reflective practitioner*. London: Jossey-Bass.

Schrag, P. (1998). New page, old lesson: Why educational standards fail the political test. *The American Prospect*, 37, 71–77.

Schumaker, D. R., & Sommers, W. A. (2001). *Being a successful principal: Riding the wave of change without drowning*. Thousand Oaks, CA: Corwin.

Schwab, J. (1969). The practical: A language for curriculum. *School Review*, 78, 1–23.

Scott, C., & Dinham, S. (2002). The beatings will continue until quality improves: Using carrots and sticks in the quest for educational improvement. *Teacher Development*, 6(1), 15–31.

Senge, P. (1990). *The fifth discipline: The art and practice of the learning organization*. New York: Doubleday.

Sergiovanni, T. J. (1998). Leadership as pedagogy, capital development and school effectiveness. *International Journal of Leadership in Education*, 1(1), 37–46.

Sergiovanni, T. J., & Starratt, R. J. (1998). *Supervision: A redefinition* (6th ed.). New York: McGraw-Hill.

Shapiro, A. (2003). *Case studies in constructivist leadership and teaching*. Lanham, MA: Scarecrow.

Sloan, K., & Sears, J. T. (Eds.) (2001). *Democratic curriculum theory & practice: Retrieving public spaces*. Troy, NY: Educator's International Press.

Smit, P. (2003). Women, mentoring, and opportunity in higher education: A South African experience. In F. K. Kochan & J. T. Pascarelli (Eds.), *Global perspectives on mentoring: Transforming contexts, communities, and cultures* (pp. 129–148). (Series: *Perspectives in mentoring, II*). Greenwich, CT: Information Age.

Smith, B. (2004). Leave no college student behind. *Multicultural Education*, 11(3), 48–49.

Smith, L. S., McAllister, L. E., & Crawford, C. S. (2001). Mentoring benefits and issues for public health nurses. *Public Health Nursing*, 18(2), 101–107.

Smith, P. L., & Smits, S. J. (1994). The feminization of leadership? *Training & Development*, 48(2), 43–46.

Smits, H. (1997). Reflection and its (dis)content(s): Re-thinking the nature of reflective practice in teacher education. *Journal of Professional Studies, 4*(2), 15–28.

Smylie, M. (1997). Research on teacher leadership: Assessing the state of the art. In B. J. Biddle (Ed.), *International handbook of teachers and teaching* (pp. 521–592). Netherlands: Kluwer Academic.

Snyder, K. M., & Acker-Hocevar, M. (2003). Building international cultures of synergy through online social networks. In F. K. Kochan & J. T. Pascarelli (Eds.), *Global perspectives on mentoring: Transforming contexts, communities, and cultures* (pp. 311–334). (Series: *Perspectives in mentoring, II*). Greenwich, CT: Information Age.

Steinberg, S. R., & Kincheloe, J. L. (1997a). Introduction: No more secrets—kinderculture, information saturation, and the postmodern childhood. In S. R. Steinberg & J. L. Kincheloe (Eds.), *Kinderculture: The corporate construction of childhood* (pp. 1–30). Boulder, CO: Westview.

Steinberg, S. R., & Kincheloe, J. L. (1997b). *Kinderculture: The corporate construction of childhood*. Boulder, CO: Westview.

Stiggins, R. J. (2002). Assessment crisis: The absence of assessment for learning. *Phi Delta Kappan, 83*(10), 758–765.

Tenner, E. (2004, August 13). The pitfalls of academic mentorships. *Chronicle of Higher Education, 50*(49), B7-B10.

Tharp, R. G., & Gallimore, R. G. (1995/1988). *Rousing minds to life: Teaching, learning, and schooling in social context*. New York: Cambridge University Press.

Tighe, E., Wang, A., & Foley, E. (2002, February). *An analysis of the effect of Children Achieving on student achievement in Philadelphia elementary schools*. Philadelphia, PA: Consortium for Policy Research in Education, 1–48. [Online]. Retrieved on September 7, 2004 from http://www.cpre.org/Publications/Children06.pdf

Twale, D. J., & Kochan, F. K. (2000). Assessment of an alternative cohort model for part-time students in an educational leadership program. *Journal of School Leadership, 10*(2), 188–208.

Tyler, R. (1949). *Basic principles of curriculum and instruction*. Chicago, IL: University of Chicago Press.

U.S. Department of Education. (2002, January 16). *No Child Left Behind Act of 2001*. Washington, DC: Office of Elementary and Secondary Education. [Online]. Retrieved on July 1, 2004 from http://www.ed.gov/policy/elsec/leg/esea02/107–110.pdf.

Voltaire, F. M. (1956). Candide, or optimism. In H. M. Block (Ed.), *Candide and other writings* (pp. 110–189). New York: Random House.

Waite, D., Boone, M., & McGhee, M. (2001). A critical sociocultural view of accountability. *Journal of School Leadership, 11*(3), 182–203.

Wang, J., Strong, M., & Odell, S. J. (2004). Mentor-novice conversations about teaching: A comparison of two U.S. and two Chinese cases. *Teachers College Record, 106*(4), 775–813.

Wellington, S. (2001). *Be your own mentor: Strategies from top women on the secrets of success.* New York: Random House Publishing Group.

Wenger, E. (1998). *Communities of practice: Learning, meaning, and identity.* New York: Cambridge University Press.

Wheatley, M. J. (1999). *Leadership and the new science: Discovering order in a chaotic world.* San Francisco, CA: Barrett-Koehler.

Wiburg, K. M. (2003). Technology and the new meaning of educational equity. *Computers in the Schools, 20*(1/2), 113–128.

Wilson, P. P., Pereira, A., & Valentine, D. (2002). Perceptions of new social work faculty about mentoring experiences. *Journal of Social Work Education, 38*(2), 317–333.

Witte, J. E., & James, W. B. (1998). Cohort partnerships: A pragmatic approach to doctoral research. *New Directions for Adult and Continuing Education, 79*, 53–62.

Wood, D. R., & Hicks, M. A. (2002). Loosening the bonds of conventionalism: Problems and possibilities of a transformative pedagogy. *Teacher Development, 6*(1), 89–104.

Young, J. P., Alvermann, D., Kaste, J., Henderson, S., & Many, J. (2004). Being a friend and a mentor at the same time: A pooled case comparison. *Mentoring & Tutoring, 12*(1), 23–36.

Zachary, L. J. (2000). *The mentor's guide: Facilitating effective learning relationships.* San Francisco, CA: Jossey-Bass.

Nonprint Resources

The following is a list of associations and organizations that function as major resource conduits providing Internet-accessible information on mentoring theory and practice and in various professional domains. While these agencies highlight education at all levels, they are especially valuable resources for K–12 schooling and are generally relevant for scholarly inquiry, mentoring application, program development, and policy implementation. The represented ideological positions range from the technical, or technocratic, to alternative, or countercultural, with a comprehensive blend emerging in the bibliographic collections.

AERA's Mentorship and Mentoring Practices SIG (Special Interest Group), Washington, DC

Purpose: "To foster mentoring programs and experiences, initiating research on the topic and providing networking and support."

Description: Provides "a forum within AERA for the involvement of individuals drawn together by a common interest in a field of study, teaching, or research when the existing divisional structure may not directly facilitate such activity."

Website: http://www.aera.net/pubs/er/pdf/v0132_05/AERA320510.pdf

Animating Mentoring Institute, Ottawa, ON

Purpose: "Partners in Practice is a national nonprofit organization with a mandate to promote mentoring in early childhood practice."

Description: Website provides information, support, and resources that encourage quality mentoring. Discusses support for balancing theory and practice through application, specifically building infrastructure for mentoring programs.

Website: www.cccf-fcsge.ca; Partners in Practice program (see report, "Partners in Mentoring"); http://www.cccffcsge.ca/practice/professional%20development/partnr_en.html

American Educational Research Association (AERA), Washington, DC

Purpose: "Concerned with the improvement of educational research and practice through the conduct of scholarly inquiry and the dissemination of information and ideas related to education. . . members are committed to act affirmatively in support of open inquiry and social justice [and to continue] deepening the appreciation of education research in sound policymaking at the federal and state levels."

Description: Mentoring-based programs and opportunities vary each year and are sponsored by Divisions A, C, and K, as well as councils on ethnic and gender equity. The focus across programs is on new scholar mentoring for doctoral students and faculty.

Website: http://www.aera.net (search term "mentor")

Association for Supervision and Curriculum Development (ASCD), Alexandria, VA

Purpose: To build "a diverse, international community of educators, forging covenants in teaching and learning for the success of all learners."

Description: Highlights education topics that include *mentoring* (search term "mentor"). These "short multimedia lessons . . . interest all levels of educators. Each lesson includes a definition, short articles on the topic, audio and video files of experts and practitioners, and a listing of resources."

Journal articles and how-to books on mentoring (http://www.ascd.org/infocon) include *Educational Leadership, Curriculum/Technology Quarterly,* and the *Journal of Curriculum and Supervision* (text summaries only).

Website: http://www.ascd.org/cms/index.cfm?TheViewID=350

Clearinghouse on Educational Policy and Management, University of Oregon, OR

> *Purpose:* To "provide information about recent major issues, trends, and topics in educational management. The information is grouped under major topics."
>
> *Description:* Journal articles, abstracts, and full text linkages are available for each topic area. Resources related to mentoring feature the series Trends and Issues. Two relevant threads are *Instructional Personnel* [Support for Beginning Teachers] and *Administrator Training*. Related mentoring topics include the role of school leader, school organization, and school reform.
>
> *Website:* eric.uoregon.edu/trends_issues

Connect with Others (fieldwork.com)

> *Purpose:* Establishing how one goes about "starting a study group from ground zero."
>
> *Description:* "Study groups are a good way to build your skills with people of similar interests in your area." Uses a threaded discussion format involving respondents (mostly college students) engaged in the characteristics of study groups as well as the advantages and disadvantages. Explicitly uses Peter Senge's learning organizations framework and filed-based texts for generating discussion within school-and-university contexts.
>
> *Website:* http://www.fieldbook.com/Study_groups/studygroupsHow.html

Connecting Generations: Intergenerational Initiative, Southern Illinois University, IL

> *Purpose:* "To promote quality education for all ages through intergenerational efforts and lifelong learning [and] a renewed commitment to citizenship with greater individual responsibility for the education of others, understanding of diverse cultures, and more active participation in education by students of all ages."
>
> *Description:* Extensive intergenerational mentoring and tutoring programs are offered for K–8 students and college freshmen that integrate both educational- and community-based stakeholders. Various nonprint publications (e.g., manuals), such as *Aging Across the Curriculum*, are available.
>
> *Website:* http://www.siu.edu/offices/iii/intg.html; mentoring and tutoring programs: http://www.siu.edu/offices/iii/model_I.html#mentoring; http://www.siu.edu/offices/iii/intg.html

European Mentoring & Coaching Council (EMCC), Europe

> *Purpose:* "Exists to promote good practice and the expectation of good practice in mentoring and coaching across Europe."
>
> *Description:* The annual conference brings together scholars and practitioners from European business, education, and the community at large. Bibliographic collections are available of articles, books, manuals, and other resources for mentoring and coaching.
>
> *Website:* http://www.emccouncil.org/frames/aboutframe.htm; librarian assistance: library@emccouncil.org.

References and Resources

International Mentoring Association, Kalamazoo, MI
> *Purpose:* To assist with "creat[ing] a highly effective mentoring program, develop and support quality mentoring practice, increase retention, learning, and performance, and build a more productive learning organization."
>
> *Description:* Includes articles, best practice models, research, websites, and links (e.g., resources for mentoring in specific settings, such as the arts, education, and government, and resources for mentoring program information relevant to all settings, such as assessment of participants, leadership issues, mentor-protégé configurations). Provides "The Mentoring Body of Knowledge," a web-based bibliography that codifies "literature on mentoring and its impact on performance of people and organizations."
>
> *Website:* http://www.mentoring-association.org

Mentoring Leadership & Resource Network (MLRN), subsidiary network of the ASCD, Alexandria, VA
> *Purpose:* "To provide an organizational vehicle for a mentoring initiative; increase the knowledge base and general awareness of best practices in the mentoring and induction of new teachers . . . promote and provide effective training for new teacher mentors; establish mentoring of new teachers as the norm in schools; and establish, through mentoring, the norms of collegiality, collaboration and continuous professional development in schools."
>
> *Description:* A grassroots network that sponsors practical issues of national and international interest concerned with teacher mentoring and induction programs. Publishes articles that members write in *Mentor*, the network's journal, which has utility for school programs.
>
> *Website:* http://www.mentors.net/03about.html

Mentoring USA or MUSA, New York, NY
> *Purpose:* Mentoring USA (or MUSA) believes that mentorship makes a difference to children in need and that "structured, one-to-one mentoring" gives them the chance for success. Targets "at risk" populations: "young children who are at risk of educational failure, children in foster care, children who have been involved with the juvenile justice system, and children who have been homeless or have recently immigrated to this country."
>
> *Description:* Builds on research and stories of experience to verify that "those children who succeed, despite often-enormous personal, economic or societal obstacles, do so because of the presence in their lives of caring, competent adults who believe in them. MUSA's goal is to supply such links to children before it is too late, in the form of early, consistent, frequent and supported attention by trained adult mentors."
>
> Coordinates three programs: (1) *General Program*—serves youth 5–13 years of age; *English as a Second Language (ESL)*—targets youth aged 9–12 years old but serves youth 9–18 years of age; and *Foster Care*—serves youth 5–18 years old in the foster care system.
>
> *Websites:* http://www.mentoringusa.org; http://www.mentoringusa.org/index1.htm

Mentor: National Mentoring Partnership, Alexandria, VA
> *Purpose:* To "advocate for the expansion of mentoring and a resource for mentors and mentoring initiatives nationwide."
>
> *Description:* Aims to foster comprehensive efforts at expanding mentoring and its impact on future generations. Committed to developing state-level mentoring partnerships that mobilize local control with participation (as of 2004) from the following states vis-à-vis the mentoring programs identified.
> - Alabama: Mentor Alabama
> - Arizona: Arizona Mentoring Partnership
> - California: California Governor's Mentoring Partnership
> - Colorado: Colorado Mentoring
> - Connecticut: The Connecticut Mentoring Partnership
> - Delaware: Delaware Mentoring Council
> - Florida: Florida Governor's Mentoring Initiative
> - Iowa: The Iowa Mentoring Partnership
> - Maine: The Maine Mentoring Partnership
> - Maryland: The Maryland Mentoring Partnership
> - Massachusetts: The Mass Mentoring Partnership
> - Michigan: Mentor Michigan
> - Minnesota: Mentoring Partnership of Minnesota
> - North Carolina: North Carolina Mentoring Partnership
> - Oregon: Oregon Mentors
> - Rhode Island: Rhode Island Mentoring Partnership/Feinstein Mentor
> - Texas: Texas Governor's Mentoring Initiative
> - Utah: Utah Mentoring Partnership
> - Vermont: Vermont Mentoring Partnership
> - Virginia: Virginia Mentoring Partnership
> - Washington: Washington State Mentoring Partnership
>
> Downloadable research reports available (http://www.mentoring.org/resources/research/mentor_works.adp).
>
> *Website:* http://www.mentoring.org/about_us/careers.adp

MentorNet, the National Electronic Industrial Mentoring Network for Women in Engineering and Science, San José, CA
> *Purpose:* To address "the retention and success of women in engineering, science and mathematics" through an e-mentoring network committed to the vision of a full representation of female professionals in male-dominated fields.
>
> *Description:* A nonprofit mentoring network for undergraduate and graduate female students majoring in engineering, related sciences, mathematics, and technologies. This electronic forum "provides highly motivated protégés from many of the world's top colleges and universities with positive, one-on-one, email-based mentoring relationships with mentors from industry and academia. In addition, the MentorNet Community provides opportunities to connect with others from around the world who are interested in women's issues in engineering and science."

Offers three structured e-mentoring programs: (1) *One-on-One Mentoring Programs:* pairs undergraduate and graduate female students and postdocs with mentors for email-based mentoring relationships "from all 50 U.S. states and 55 countries on 6 continents"; (2) *MentorNet* E-Forum: offers web-based discussion on such topics as Work/Life Balance, Job Searching, and Graduate School; and (3) *Resources:* relevant to women in engineering and science (e.g., resume database for job-seeking or internships)
Website: http://www.mentornet.net

Menttium Corporation, Minneapolis, MN
Purpose: To work closely with "organization[s] to design and implement mentoring solutions, [and] successfully attract, develop, and retain talented people."
Description: A national consultant and corporate industry firm described as a "pioneer leader in today's mentoring models" that innovates and leads in this "burgeoning industry." Uses a "strategic approach [to deliver] powerful mentoring experiences" linked to business objectives; targeted to positively impact the performance of individual employees; and focused on the long-term viability of organizations.
An "innovative cross-company mentoring solution" that offers organizations "a cost-effective way to foster the development of talented women." The methods used vary and amount to "a unique combination of cross-geographic, cross-company mentoring, business education and networking delivered in a virtual model via leading edge technology, email and phone."
Menttium 100, a sister company, is a program for professionals of color: www.menttium.com
"News room" feature—provides short articles on the topics of executive mentoring and promoting women into authority positions: http://www.menttium.com/press.htm
Website: http://www.menttium.com/menttium.htm

National Education Association, NW Washington, DC
Purpose: "To elevate the character and advance the interests of the profession of teaching and to promote the cause of popular education in the United States."
Description: A national leader committed to advancing the cause of public education. The NEA's 2.7 million members "work at every level of education, from preschool to university graduate programs. NEA has affiliates in every state, as well as in more than 13,000 local communities across the United States."

Publications and multimedia resources: http://www.nea.org/he
Mentoring Programs in Higher Education: Provides a national map and brief description of programs offered on university campuses within many (but not all) states.
Minority Mentoring Programs in Higher Education: Both the NEA and the American Association of University Professors have released "policy statements supporting programs to improve the participation of minority stu-

dents, teachers, and faculty at all levels of education." The aim is to create mentoring opportunities to increase minority participation in higher education.

Website: http://www.nea.org/he/mentor.html

National Mentoring Center, Northwest Regional Educational Laboratory, Portland, OR

Purpose: Apply 'best practices' and standards for youth-based mentoring programs across the United States through national training and technical assistance.

Description: The Generic Mentoring Program Policy & Procedure Manual was designed for wide applicability to mentoring programs (http://www.nwrel.org/mentoring/policy_manual.html).

Website: http://www.nwrel.org/mentoring

Peer Systems Consulting Group, Victoria, BC

Purpose: To provide training, educational resources, and consultation to anyone seeking to "establish or strengthen peer helping, peer support, peer mediation, peer referral, peer education, peer coaching, and mentor programs in schools, universities, communities, and corporations."

Description: Peer-juried listings are available, along with a compendium review of mentoring resources, specifically books and articles. Includes "What's Hot—Top Mentor Publications" (http://www.peer.ca/topmenbks), as well as training manuals and how-to guides. Peer Resources publishes *Compass: The Magazine of Peer Assistance, Coaching, and Mentoring*; also makes available *The Mentor News*, in both print and nonprint (http://www.peer.ca/Compassinfo.html).

Sponsored programs: Mentor Program Leadership for Educators; Building and Maintaining a Corporate Mentoring Program

Websites: http://www.peer.ca/cgi-bin/ms2/rcarr/search; http://www.mentors.ca/trng

Tutor/Mentor Connection (T/MC), Cabrini Connections, Chicago, IL

Purpose: "To gather and organize all that is known about successful nonschool tutor/mentor programs and share that knowledge to expand the availability and enhance the effectiveness of these services to children in inner city Chicago and other poverty areas."

Description: The Tutor/Mentor Connection seeks to establish tutor/mentor programs in poorly performing schools and within poverty areas. Shares relevant information in a public awareness campaign aimed at creating a greater involvement of all adults; channels resources to individual programs; and promotes understanding of the long-term actions needed to help impoverished youth obtain a job: "For each child this is a minimum 25–year commitment."

Contains information about the tutor/mentor programs operating in the Chicago region. Offers papers and publications related to tutoring/mentoring: http://www.tutormentorexchange.net/Resources/Manuscripts.asp

Website: http://www.tutormentorexchange.net/Giving_Back/Lend_A_Hand.htm

Westchester County Office for Women, White Plains, NY

> *Purpose:* "The Westchester County Office for Women is dedicated to working for equal rights for women and the recognition of the full worth of all women." It honors Martha Sloan Greenawalt, a civic leader and role model for women.
>
> *Description:* Addresses "the needs of women and families in Westchester County on three levels: public policy and advocacy; public education and research; and direct services."
>
> The Martha Sloan Greenawalt Young Women's Mentoring Program "seeks to motivate adolescent girls to achieve their full potential by providing positive role models, social and cultural enrichment, and a supportive environment." This initiative "grew out of concern over studies that continue to report that adolescent girls lack self-esteem, self-confidence, and opportunities compared to their male peers. One of the most widely respected and effective methods of helping girls to 'reclaim' their sense of self is a mentoring relationship with a female role model."
>
> This mentoring program specifically aims to "encourage girls to develop to their fullest potential" by nurturing their self-confidence, helping them to "develop their own vision for the future, identify real leadership, and make wise choices," as well as "work with parents, schools, and communities" so that their talents can be realized and relationships better negotiated. Successful women are matched with young women who face "the challenges of adolescence."
>
> Also committed to equality and justice on behalf of Hispanic women: "Through its direct service division, the Office for Women offers domestic violence advocacy, outreach and education to Spanish speaking women through its new Hispanic Outreach/Advocacy Program." Provides domestic violence resources: http://www.westchestergov.org/women/hispanic_outreach.htm
>
> *Website:* http://www.westchestergov.org/women/mentor.htm

Peter Lang PRIMERS
in Education

Peter Lang Primers are designed to provide a brief and concise introduction or supplement to specific topics in education. Although sophisticated in content, these primers are written in an accessible style, making them perfect for undergraduate and graduate classroom use. Each volume includes a glossary of key terms and a References and Resources section.

Other published and forthcoming volumes cover such topics as:

- Standards
- Popular Culture
- Critical Pedagogy
- Literacy
- Higher Education
- John Dewey
- Feminist Theory and Education
- Studying Urban Youth Culture
- Multiculturalism through Postformalism
- Creative Problem Solving
- Teaching the Holocaust
- Piaget and Education
- Deleuze and Education
- Foucault and Education

Look for more Peter Lang Primers to be published soon. To order other volumes, please contact our Customer Service Department:

    800-770-LANG (within the US)
    212-647-7706 (outside the US)
    212-647-7707 (fax)

To find out more about this and other Peter Lang book series, or to browse a full list of education titles, please visit our website:
    www.peterlangusa.com

www.ingramcontent.com/pod-product-compliance
Ingram Content Group UK Ltd.
Pitfield, Milton Keynes, MK11 3LW, UK
UKHW021846140426
5217IPUK00022B/1625